Angels

ANGELS

Messengers of Grace

❖

Martin Israel

First published in Great Britain 1995
Society for Promoting Christian Knowledge
Holy Trinity Church
Marylebone Road
London NW1 4DU

Biblical quotations are from the *Revised English Bible* © 1989
Oxford and Cambridge University Presses

British Library Cataloguing-in-Publication Data
A catalogue record for this book is available from
the British Library

ISBN 0-281-04832-0

Typeset by Latimer Trend & Company Ltd, Plymouth
Printed in Great Britain by
Redwood Books, Trowbridge, Wiltshire

Contents

◆◇◆

ACKNOWLEDGEMENTS

My thanks are due to my several friends who have been so kind as to allow me to publish accounts of their angelic visitations.

When the sun rises, do you not see a round disc of fire somewhat like a gold piece? O no, no, I see an innumerable company of the heavenly host crying 'Holy, Holy, Holy, is the Lord God Almighty.'

(William Blake, *The Vision of Judgement*)

Do not talk what thou wouldst do if thou wast an angel, but consider what thou canst do as thou art a man.

(William Law, *A Practical Treatise upon Christian Perfection*)

What a piece of work is a man! How noble in reason! how infinite in faculties! in form and moving, how express and admirable! in action, how like an angel! in apprehension, how like a god! the beauty of the world! the paragon of animals!

(William Shakespeare, *Hamlet*)

Twice or thrice had I loved thee,
Before I knew thy face or name.
So in a voice, so in a shapeless flame,
Angels affect us oft, and worshipped be.

(John Donne, *Air and Angels*)

A Dream

◆◇◆

I seemed to have been involved in a road accident, and I clambered out of a rather shadowy car. The road ahead was poorly made up, and I had to crawl my way forward – in the process, escaping from some people who were impeding my departure. At last I reached the end of the road and found myself in a vast expanse of clear space. There were no markings, but the space was occupied by diaphanous beings who had a mere outline of shape. This shape superficially resembled the human form, but there were no recognizable features. They seemed to cluster together in joyous groups, animated by a spirit of love that poured out into the atmosphere. They received me as one of their own, and I seemed to play along with them in their harmonious movement.

Then I began to wonder where I actually was. One of the company seemed to sense my question and asked me, 'Don't you know that you are dead?' I then seemed to be ushered towards a great shadowy building where someone awaited me, apparently for appraisal and instruction. By this point, though, I was so excited that I seemed to awaken myself consciously: I had had direct proof of the survival of my personality after bodily death, and I wanted to make this knowledge available to others as soon as possible. Seldom have I woken up with such excitement and joy. Shortly afterwards, I even considered writing a book on what I had experienced, but a later, more sober, consideration showed that there was barely enough material for even a single page of foolscap.

Nevertheless, this dream has played its part in writing this book, for the diaphanous ones whom I saw were certainly angels. Who it was that I was to visit I can only conjecture. I had absolute trust and confidence that all was well, and so it may have been a representative of God the Holy Trinity. Had I been rather less impetuous, I might conceivably have attained this knowledge, but I suspect I did what was expected of me.

A Dream

In my earthly state of spiritual understanding, I am surely not eligible for a heavenly meeting. It may be that when I make the great transition that we call death I shall be better prepared for what is to come.

The object of this book is to establish the angels in their place as ministers of God's grace to his manifold creatures. I have concentrated only peripherally on actual apparitions, because these are well recorded in the considerable contemporary literature on angels; instead, my interest has centred more on their nature and function in the divine economy. However one views the origin of angels, it seems quite certain that they are an essential link between a human being and God – and, more universally, between the whole created world and its creator. It will be an important day when theologians decide to give the matter more attention, for then they will come closer to the divine source.

I

Angels in a Mystical Context

❖❖❖

'God is light, and in him there is no darkness at all,' writes St John in his first letter (1 John 1.5). The problem of God's existence, let alone his purposeful activity in the world, never ceases to excite the speculations of the philosopher and the heated disgust of the many humans who suffer abominably at the hands of their fellow creatures no less than as a result of the various natural disasters that rock the earth. The God of theistic religion so often seems to be either vicious or else incompetent. There are episodes in the early part of the Old Testament that would seem to substantiate God's viciousness, while the intolerable calamities that have punctuated human history would point to divine carelessness, if not frank cruelty. It is not easy to justify a constructive divine existence on purely intellectual grounds.

But it is not with the reason that God is primarily known. There is an even more powerful seat of recognition, which is traditionally called the soul – the point of a person's true identity. The enigmatic words of *The Cloud of Unknowing*, a mystical treatise of unknown authorship from the fourteenth century, speak volumes: 'But now thou askest me, "How shall I think on Himself, and what is He?" Unto this I cannot answer thee. I wot now that thou hast brought me into the same cloud of unknowing that I would thou wert in thyself. But this I would say "By love He may be gotten and holden, but by thought never."'[1] The writer of this work was a great mystic, a term which is used to describe someone apparently granted a direct awareness of the divine presence, so that he or she is filled with the divine light of illumination as well as the divine heat of love. Such a person is inwardly changed, and by their presence brings fresh hope and understanding to people around them, who are then open to a new vision of reality. 'You will recognize them by their fruit' (Matthew 7.16) is a very sound canon of judgement.

Reading the works of the great mystics fills any receptive person with a joy of recognition that leaps out of the darkness of worldly agnosticism and lights up the way of love, joy and peace. What was always known in the depths of the soul is now confirmed in the life of the person, who can then proceed with hope and love. It would seem that the direct awareness of the God who transcends all human understanding lights up the divine spark within all humans, so that they may go forward through the darkness of intellectual doubt to the light of a new day, where loving concern will work in concert with an enlightened reason. The end is a growing wisdom that inspires the whole world with a dynamic concept of God in all things, as a reflection of the God beyond all names, whose essence is sometimes best expressed in purely negative terms.

There are two types of knowledge: the rational and the mystical. The first type follows the capacity of the mind to synthesize data received from the senses or learned by communication from other sources. As such, the mind can attain mastery over the tangible world to the extent of changing once-familiar landmarks. We are all aware of how modern technology has changed the face of our earth. We hope that such changes will work out for the good of everyone in the end, but at times the concomitant destruction may also cause a pang of regret. This is what is entailed in rational progress. In contrast, mystical knowledge is of an entirely different order. It not only stills the rational mind, but it also brings to light a new, or at least undiscovered, part of the person that was previously concealed by a dominating, arrogant reasoning mind that naively believed it was the source of all wisdom. With mystical knowledge, one knows by direct experience that into which one is unceremoniously immersed: it is in the darkness of complete ignorance that a very different approach to reality is opened up.

This is the knowledge that St Paul writes about in Ephesians 3.17–19. In a glorious prayer he appeals, 'With deep roots and firm foundations may you, in company with all God's people, be strong to grasp what is the breadth and length and height and depth of Christ's love, and to know it, though it is beyond knowledge.' This knowledge cannot be attained by an act of the will, for it is a spontaneous experience of God's grace in its highest dispensation. It comes to those who are ready to receive it, according to the divine judgement and not by human striving; and once it is known, a very different understanding of the human journey is set before us. We can repeat the words, 'by love he may be gotten and holden, but by thought never', with a new understanding: this love is a complete emptying of oneself so that the divine energies can pour through one, and so that one can say with Isaiah, after his shattering vision in the Temple, 'Here am I! Send me' (Isaiah 6.9).

The result of such mystical enlightenment is that the will is reformed so that it becomes aligned to the divine will, and one works in a spirit of love that gives itself in compassion to all that lives: 'I have been crucified with Christ: the life I now live is not my life, but the life which Christ lives in me; and my present mortal life is lived by faith in the Son of God, who loved me and gave himself up for me' (Galatians 2.20). The ego has indeed been crucified, and the true self, or soul, can begin to learn something of a real life that far exceeds the limitations of the rational mind, without in any way failing to concede its place in dealing with the things of this world. 'Pay Caesar what belongs to Caesar, and God what belongs to God' (Mark 12.17). The true mystic is a very practical person, bringing the energies of God down to the world.

Yet between the triune Godhead (Father, Son, and Holy Spirit) and creation – the mystically dominant and the physically ebullient – there exists an order of beings that is spiritual in nature, but able to convey the divine energies to all that lives. These beings are the angels, an angel being a messenger; and the message conveyed by this order of spiritual beings is the light of God, for God himself/herself is known to us by his/her outflowing energies, love and uncreated light. (We need to remember that personal pronouns limit our means of communicating information about the ineffable One who is assuredly beyond gender, and yet obviously is involved in gender through being the creator of all that exists. Having made this observation, I will use the masculine pronoun in order to keep the language succinct.) The light of God is the way of spiritual illumination, and in the universe it is the origin of the light that comes from the sun and other stars. This is the light recorded in Genesis 1.3.

One great mystic who wrote between AD 475 and 525 used the pseudonym Dionysius the Areopagite, after one of the few converts St Paul made during his frustrating visit to Athens (Acts 17.34). His treatise entitled *On Mystical Theology* (a more recent translation is entitled *The Mystical Theology*) is a classical dissertation on the workings of the mystical consciousness at the most profound level. Only a few pages long, it is a brilliant exposition of the apophatic way of knowing God, which has been the keystone in the teaching of many subsequent mystics, including the writer of *The Cloud of Unknowing* and St John of the Cross (1542–91). The apophatic way of knowledge uses 'negatives' – that is, it describes who God is by saying what he is *not*. Another, rather longer, work of the 'pseudo-Dionysius' is *On Celestial Hierarchies*, or *The Celestial Hierarchies*,[2] in which he describes at length the hierarchy of angelic beings – nine orders in all, ranging from the seraphim and cherubim, who are nearest to God, to the angels, who are closest to the world. The illumination of the pseudo-Dionysius was the basis of this final categorization of the angelic hierarchy, but much of it was known to the Fathers of the Christian Church. A number of the categories appear in the Bible and in some Jewish apocryphal writings, notably the Book of Enoch.

A hierarchy is defined by Dionysius as a holy order which, so far as attainable, participates in the Divine Likeness. He goes on to observe that each of those who is allotted a place in the Divine Order finds his perfection in being uplifted, according to his capacity, towards the Divine Likeness; and what is still more divine, he becomes, as the Scriptures say, a fellow-worker with God, showing forth the Divine Activity revealed as far as possible in himself. For the holy constitution of the hierarchy ordains that some are purified, others purify; some are enlightened, others enlighten; some are perfected, others make perfect; for in this way the divine imitation will fit each one. A glorious climax is attained in this mystical observation:

4

Inasmuch as the Divine Bliss (to speak in human terms) is exempt from all dissimilarity, and is full of Eternal Light, perfect, in need of no perfection, purifying, illuminating, perfecting, being rather Himself the holy Purification, Illumination and Perfection, above purification, above light, supremely perfect, Himself the origin of perfection and the cause of every hierarchy, He transcends in excellence all holiness.

The great influences on Dionysius are clearly Holy Scripture and the writings of the neo-Platonic mystics Plotinus and his disciple Proclus.

Dionysius, by systematizing the nine orders of the angelic hierarchy, makes them more accessible to us. As a mystic he deplores the tendency to express spiritual essences in material forms. This is called reification, but in the end he accepts both its necessity for purposes of general intellectual communication and its validity inasmuch as the creatures of the world mirror the beauty of their creator. Dionysius reminds us that the theology of the Bible includes such symbols as the Sun of Justice, the Morning Star rising mystically in the mind, or the Light shining forth unclouded and intelligibly to celebrate the deity itself. 'So the Word became flesh; he made his home among us, and we saw his glory, such glory as befits the Father's only Son, full of grace and truth' (John 1.14). In this famous statement we see a perfect apposition of the material and the spiritual.

The angelic beings, or celestial intelligences, are divided into three triads, containing the nine orders, and whose names, as we shall see, represent the divine attributes that they manifest to all below them. Continuing from the fine introduction to the work, Dionysius says these divine attributes also have an inner relation with every human soul, for through their ministrations the aspiring soul becomes liberated from the bondage of material things, receives knowledge of that soul's purpose, and is enabled to live its true life, ultimately attaining its divine likeness to the full.

The first order of the first triad is *seraphim*. They are described in the passage already quoted from Isaiah as the 'burning' or 'fiery' ones, from whom the stream of superessential grace flows (God transcends all essence). Like fire, the seraphim consume all that separates the human from God. The second order is *cherubim*. The name 'cherub' means 'fullness of knowledge'. Through cherubim, the energy of God streams forth as a transcendental light that perfectly illuminates the soul and unites it with the divine wisdom. It imparts a full and lucid understanding to the universal divine immanence. In the Bible, cherubs are depicted as great winged creatures – for instance, in the construction of the Ark in the wilderness (Exodus 25.18 *passim*), King Solomon's majestic temple (1 Kings 6.23 *passim*), and the visions of Ezekiel (Ezekiel 1.10 and 10.1 *passim*). In one passage, the cherub is portrayed as a flying creature on which God travelled in order to help King David (2 Samuel 22.11). All this shows how hard it is for the human mind to avoid conceptualizing a formless energy. The third order of the first triad are the *thrones*; these are divine seats through which the soul is lifted up to God and becomes established in the constancy of the divine service. This first triad is closest at all times to the divine presence.

In the second triad come first the *dominions*, or *dominations*, that are free from all earthly passions, from all inward inclination to the bondage of discord, and from all that is low; they display a liberal superiority to harsh tyranny, and an exemptness from degrading servility. They are true lords, perpetually aspiring to true lordship, and to the Source of Lordship. The second order of the second triad are the *virtues*, that have a powerful and unshakeable virility welling forth into all their God-like energies. There is no weakness in them: instead, they ascend unwaveringly to the superessential virtue which is the Source of Virtue, and flow forth providentially to those below. The third order are the *powers*, or *authorities*, that are invested with a capacity to regulate intellectual and supermundane power which never debases its authority by tyrannical force, but is irresistibly urged onward in due order to the Divine. This order beneficently leads those below it, as far as possible, to the supreme power which is the Source of Power. It re-directs the forces that fetter the human mind to earthly things. Through this second triad, the soul is liberated from all that is below, and assimilated to that which is above.

The third, and lowest, triad is concerned with the final execution of the work of providence, which is God's beneficent care for his creatures. The *principalities* exhibit divine lordship and true service; through them, the soul may turn from attachment to earthly activities to the service of God, so as ultimately to become a co-worker with the divine ministers. The *archangels* imprint the divine seal on all things, whereby the universe is the written word of God. They impart to the soul the spiritual light through which it may learn to read the Bible, and also to know and use its own faculties correctly. The lowest order of this triad is the *angels*, who minister to all things of nature, including humans, by purifying and uplifting them.

In this triadic scheme, the higher orders inspire those lower than they, but not vice versa. Thus it is clear that the third triad is nearest the world, and transmits the illumination received from above. The end of the process is the transfiguration of the whole of the universe in the glorious light that proceeds from on high. This whole hierarchy spreads the divine light through the cosmos, that vast realm that includes the universe, as far as human understanding can define it, and also the psychic plane where we may meet the spirits of the dead and also the communion of saints and the ministry of angels. The great work of the angelic hierarchy is to praise and glorify God. This praise is not a rational acclaim so much as a great paean of joy that the world is as it is and that the angels are privileged both to know it and to participate in it. This is how we should say the Gloria of the Eucharist: that we are privileged to partake of the body and blood of the Saviour. If the whole cosmos could resound to that praise, and move beyond prejudice and emotional bonds, we would pour out peace and goodwill to all creatures. The angelic hierarchy, with its enlightened will turned resolutely to the divine presence, helps to bring forward the Kingdom of God on earth – and elsewhere in our unimaginably glorious cosmos.

And so it is that all aspiring human souls move to the divine presence, aided by an immense angelic hierarchy, none more important than the other. If the humble angel leads the way, the destination is through the cherub and seraph to the source of all being whom we call God. It may well be that much illumination from the Holy Spirit comes to us through the angelic hierarchy, centring on our own guardian angel. (This is something we will consider later.) One thing is certain, though: we must worship the Holy Trinity and no other power.

In this respect, it is noteworthy that St Paul entertains a decidedly critical view of the angelic hierarchy. Thus in his two most mystical letters, those to the Ephesians and the Colossians, he proceeds at length to stress the superiority of Christ to any heavenly potentate. Christ is indeed, apart from being incarnate as the man Jesus, also the Cosmic Christ. All other powers in this vast realm are at the very least subordinate to him; at the worst, they may embrace evil tendencies. Speaking of the Father in Ephesians 1.19–21, Paul writes, 'His mighty strength was seen at work when he raised Christ from the dead, and enthroned him at his right hand in the heavenly realms, far above all government and authority, all power and dominion, and any title of sovereignty that commands allegiance, not only in this age but also in the age to come.' In the Authorized Version, the angelic connation is even more decisive: '... far above all principality, and power, and might, and dominion.' In Ephesians 6.12, St Paul is even more explicit: 'For our struggle is not against human foes, but against cosmic powers, against the authorities and potentates of this dark age, against the superhuman forces of evil in the heavenly realms.' A different image is portrayed in Colossians 2.15: 'There he disarmed the cosmic powers and authorities and made a public spectacle of them, leading them as captives in his triumphal procession.' This warning is especially pertinent in present times, when many listen to all manner of communications purporting to come from high sources in the cosmic realm. The judgement on such sources should always be: do these communications lead the hearer to a more Christ-like frame of mind that shows itself in positive action in the world around, or are they merely messages of complacency leading to self-satisfaction?

The nature of angels is still debatable. They appear to be spiritual agents with an independent will, who obey the directive of the one who sent them on their errand. Though normally invisible, they are capable of assuming a corporeal form, even appearing as humans on special occasions. They are what the parapsychologist would term 'idioplastic' — that is, capable of assuming a number of appearances. They represent a distinct line of cosmic evolution that is unrelated to the human species; that is, a human cannot develop into an angel. Yet one thing seems certain: the human, though of a lower order than the angels, has the prospect of a far higher development. Christ assumed a human form, not an angelic one. The unknown author of the Letter to Hebrews stresses this in the first chapter of this fine work. There is something about the complete freedom of action of the fully integrated person that brings them closely into the divine presence: 'When he had brought about purification from sins, he took his seat at the right hand of God's Majesty on high, raised as far above the angels as the title he has inherited is superior to theirs' (Hebrews 1.3–4).

The angelic group, for all its exaltation, has probably reached the peak of its development. On the other hand, humans, incomplete though they may appear spiritually, have a capacity for infinite growth, so that the spark of God in the soul may eventually blaze forth into a glorious Christ-like presence. In the Hindu tradition, the same observations seem to apply to the *devas*, the angelic beings of that religion. They do not progress beyond what they are, though there may be a cyclical type of development. In the Buddhist faith, the angelic beings are called *nats*, many of which are nature spirits. In Tibetan Buddhism there are rather move elevated angelic beings called *dakini* (a Sanskrit word) or *khadroma* (the analagous Tibetan word).

It is evident that angelic beings are encountered in all the great world faiths, but it is in the monotheistic group (Judaism, Christianity, and Islam) that they play an especially prominent part. This may be due to the emphatically transcendent view of God that is native to these three religions. The angelic hierarchy may act as a bridge between God and his vast creation, or at least

2

Angels in the Old Testament

❖❖❖

The Bible describes the action of angels on numerous occasions, but there is no established doctrine about them other than simply their presence in the relationship between God and his creation. Right from the beginning of creation, angels are not so much described, as their presence noted. In the allegory of the Fall, where two prototype humans disobey the command of God not to eat the fruit of the tree of the knowledge of good and evil, a part of Adam's and Eve's fearsome punishment is total exclusion from paradise: 'When he drove him out, God settled him to the east of the garden of Eden, and he stationed the cherubim and a sword whirling and flashing to guard the way to the tree of life' (Genesis 3.24). I believe that this episode is far better understood as a myth, a spiritual truth recounted in terms of symbols, than as an historical fact. In the equally tragic story of Cain and Abel in Genesis 4, Cain is given a special mark of protection lest anyone should kill him in his solitary journey. This would seem to indicate the existence of an established group who might threaten Cain's life, an impossibility if he and his parents Adam and Eve were the sole inhabitants of the earth.

In fact, the Fall is a universal occurrence in the lives of us all, when we are obliged to quit the unreflecting safety of infancy and enter upon the experience of childhood and adult life, fighting our own way in a milieu of rivalry and conflicting spiritual values. The end of this perilous journey is the development of the free will, so that with courage and integrity we may claim entrance to the paradise we were obliged to leave as growing children. In the beginning we had received God's love without acknowledgement, while now we can, (indeed, have to), reciprocate that love in our own lives; we love because he loved us first (1 John 4.19).

More intimate experiences of angels occur later on in the story of Abraham and his descendants. Thus Hagar, Sarah's slave-girl, is first encouraged to cohabit with Abraham because Sarah is apparently barren and growing old. However, Hagar treated her mistress with contempt when she became pregnant, and was summarily dismissed from her post. As Hagar walks disconsolately in the wilderness, we are told that the angel of God appears to her and promises her a great future; yet first she has to return to Sarah and endure her ill-treatment. Soon afterwards, three holy men visit the home of Abraham, who shows them great hospitality. They foretell the birth of Isaac, a physical impossibility in view of Sarah's advanced years, and then they take Abraham with them to Sodom and Gomorrah, two cities riddled with vice. When the men, who by now have revealed their true identity as angels of high degree, go towards Sodom, Abraham debates with the Lord the fate of these two accursed cities. It is noteworthy that these angels are often called the angels of the Lord; at an earlier period, they are identified with God himself, but later they are regarded as special messengers of the Deity. It is of interest how in Genesis 18 the interplay between the three angels and God is subtly interwoven. Thus the angels announce future events to Abraham, while he himself is privileged to have direct access to the Lord, and to debate with him the extent of destruction in store for Sodom and Gomorrah: even ten just men found in the cities would be sufficient to save them from ruin. Abraham's question is eternally relevant, 'Will you really sweep away innocent and wicked together?' (Genesis 18.23).

In Genesis 19, the denouement is described: two of the angels visit Lot's house (he is Abraham's brother) in Sodom, where they excite the lust of the male population. These are successfully parried, and the angels urge Lot to flee with his family at once; he escapes to a small town called Zoar, from whence he moves on with his two daughters to a cave in the hill country. Abraham witnesses the destruction of the two towns from a distance. The penultimate angelic visit in the Abrahamic story occurs in Genesis 21: Isaac is conceived and born to Sarah, but later she is affronted by the sight of his playing with Ishmael, Hagar's son. Once again, the servant-girl is driven out into the wilderness, and when all seems hopeless for the child, the angel of the Lord comes to give her support, promising that Ishmael will become a great nation. God then opens Hagar's eyes and she sees a well full of water. God was indeed with Ishmael as he grew up, for he is the ancestor of the Arab people. The final appearance of angels in the story of Abraham occurs in Genesis 22.11–12, when an angel prevents Abraham's sacrifice of his son Isaac.

Jacob, Abraham's grandson, is visited by angels after his dispute with Esau, his twin brother. Jacob fled; eventually he came to a shrine, where he stopped for the night. Using a stone as a pillow, he lay down and slept. Then came Jacob's famous dream: he saw a ladder that rested on the ground with its top reaching heaven, and the angels of God were going up and down it. The Lord was standing beside him saying, 'I am the Lord, the God of your father Abraham and the God of Isaac. The land on which you are lying I shall give to you and your descendants' (Genesis 28.13). The end of the message is especially encouraging, and has heartened many people of later times: 'I shall not leave you until I have done what I have promised you' (Genesis 28.15). Jacob had a further encounter with angels later on, and he called the place Mahanaim (Genesis 32.1–2). Yet what are we to make of the famous encounter he had on his return to Canaan, fleeing from his predatory uncle Laban and fearful of the revenge of his now powerful brother, Esau? The whole incident has an atmospheric quality that is worth recording (Genesis 32.22–31):

> During the night Jacob rose, and taking his two wives, his two slave-girls, and his eleven sons, he crossed the ford of Jabbok. After he had sent them across the wadi with all that he had, Jacob was left alone, and a man wrestled with him there till daybreak. When the man saw that he could not get the better of Jacob, he struck him in the hollow of his thigh, so that Jacob's hip was dislocated as they wrestled. The man said, 'Let me go, for day is breaking,' but Jacob replied, 'I will not let you go unless you bless me.' The man asked, 'What is your name?' 'Jacob,' he answered. The man said, 'Your name shall no longer be Jacob but Israel, because

you have striven with God and with mortals, and have prevailed.' Jacob said, 'Tell me your name, I pray.' He replied, 'Why do you ask my name?' but he gave him his blessing there. Jacob called the place Peniel, 'because,' he said, 'I have seen God face to face yet my life is spared.' The sun rose as Jacob passed through Peniel, limping because of his hip.

It is highly unlikely that this assailant was God himself, but instead was an angel of God; for no one can see God directly and remain alive, a fact on which all mystics would agree. The morally ambivalent nature of the assailant is even more stunning, there being an almost demonic aspect to the attack. On the other hand, Jacob deserved it; his own morally ambivalent behaviour to Esau and Laban was turned sharply upon himself, but he proved himself to be a man of courage, which fully compensated for his moral ambiguity. The name 'Israel' is best translated 'may God show his strength'.

A comparable enigmatic encounter is described in Exodus 4.24–6, when the Lord met Moses, whom he had already chosen for his great commission of delivering the Israelites from Egyptian slavery. Moses was on a journey and encamped for the night, and the Lord 'would have killed him' (verse 24). Moses' wife Zipporah performed an emergency circumcision, and so 'the Lord let Moses alone' (verse 26). It is easy enough to dismiss these encounters as primitive views of God's transcendence, but I suspect a profound knowledge of God's majesty is enshrined in them. We cannot call God to account if we fail to obey the Law; his angel can exact a stern penalty.

In the course of the Israelite exodus from Egypt, angels play an unobtrusive yet constant role: 'And now I am sending an angel before you to guard you on your way and to bring you to the place I have prepared' (Exodus 23.20). Similar thoughts are found in Exodus 23.23, 32.34 and 33.2. Numbers 20.16 reiterates this theme, but the story of Balaam and Balak brings the work of angels into stronger relief (Numbers 22–4). The Moabite king summons the seer Balaam to curse the menacing Israelite hordes approaching his land. First of all, Balaam consults God, and is told not to obey this request; he remains at home, but a subsequent delegation from Balak leads to God instructing him to go with the Moabite chiefs to Balak. Now, strangely, God is angry with Balaam for going to meet the king, and installs his angel in the path of Balaam's ass to obstruct its way. The animal's perverse action infuriates the seer, until he is told directly by the animal that it is the angel of the Lord who is obstructing his passage. Then Balaam's eyes are opened so that he too can see the angel, who tells him to proceed to the king's service. Here, contrary to Balak's instructions, he confers a mighty blessing on the Israelites according to the will of God, and much to Balak's fury. Afterwards, both men go their respective ways. The story has features in common with a fairy-tale, notably the ass's sudden gift of speech, but it teaches us that God's will cannot be thwarted, no matter how capricious this may appear to be, and that he works in our world through the ministry of angels.

At the beginning of the Book of Judges (2.1–4), the angel of the Lord castigates the people for their disobedience to the Law given to Moses and their unfaithfulness to the one true God. They break out into loud lamentations, but their repentance is short-lived, a theme that runs through the Old Testament. God sends them judges, kings (at their own request, of whom David is by far the most spiritual), and later prophets, all of whom show the right way. Yet the people remain tragically fickle until the time of the Babylonian exile. A more positive visitation attends the birth of Samson, the Israelite Hercules: 'There was a certain man from Zorah of the tribe of Dan whose name was Manoah and whose wife was barren; she had no child' (Judges 13.2). Recalling the story of Abraham and Sarah, an angel of the Lord then appeared to Manoah's wife, predicting the birth of a son, who was to abstain from drinking alcohol or eating any forbidden food, for he was to be a Nazirite, consecrated to God from birth. He was destined to strike the first blow for Israelite freedom against the power of the Philistines (Judges 13.1–5). The angel assumed a human form, like the three who visited Abraham and Sarah in the story of Isaac's birth and the destruction of Sodom and Gomorrah. Not surprisingly, neither Manoah nor his wife perceived the angelic nature of their visitor (though the woman had some intimations), who refused to reveal his name, which he described as a name of wonder. When they prepared an offering to the Lord, the flame went up from the altar towards heaven and the angel of the Lord ascended in the flame. Seeing this, Manoah and his wife both 'fell face downward to the ground' (Judges 13.20). The angel of the Lord did not appear to them again (Judges 13.21).

At the end of 2 Samuel, there is the strange account of David being impelled to take a census of Judah and Israel (2 Samuel 24). In this account, God tells David to perform this action, whereas in the parallel in I Chronicles 21 the inciting agent is clearly identified as the devil (Satan). To take a census was tantamount to pre-empting God's work in providing and expanding the population of Israel. The punishment David chose was three days of pestilence in the land; and so the angel of the Lord stretched out his arm towards Jerusalem to destroy it, but fortunately the Lord repented of the evil and stopped the angel at once, who was then at the threshing-floor of Araunah the Jebusite. David bought the threshing-floor from Araunah, and built an altar on it where he made the customary offerings of that time. Then the Lord yielded to the prayer for the land, and the plague in Israel stopped.

In the period after the schism between the Northern Kingdom of Israel and the Southern Kingdom of Judah, angels play a more important role. In I Kings 13.21–2, we learn that any message transmitted by an angel is as nothing compared with the direct word of God. An angel may assuredly be the messenger of God's word whose authority remains unassailable, for it has a direct power that should never be contravened. However, an angel has no direct authority of its own; it is the power behind it that tells whether it is of God or the devil. In this particular instance, there was no angel at all, for the man in question, though a prophet, was lying to his more illustrious peer when he persuaded him to take refreshment at his home instead of returning whence he had come without any delay (I Kings 13.11–22).

Later on in the history of Israel appears the charismatic figure of Elijah; the Elijah sequence begins at I Kings 17 and continues on to much of 2 Kings 2. It was after he had destroyed the prophets of Baal, and Jezebel – the wife of King

Ahab (the patron of the cult of Baal) – had threatened him with death, that Elijah fled by stages to Mount Horeb, the same Mount Sinai that Moses had climbed some four hundred and fifty years previously. Elijah was extremely dejected, but on the way angels had provided food for his immediate survival (I Kings 19.1–9). While he was asleep in the course of his precipitate flight, an angel awakened him: and there at his head was a cake baked on hot stones and a pitcher of water. Thus Elijah ate and drank and lay down again. Then the angel of the Lord awakened him a second time, providing him with food for a forty-day journey to Horeb, the mountain of God. There Elijah entered a cave where he spent the night. On the next day, he experienced God directly as 'a faint murmuring sound' ('still small voice' in the Authorized Version). This is God as Spirit who speaks intimately to his prophets. There is no need for the preliminary cosmic events like a hurricane, an earthquake, or a fire, which acted as a prelude to the events of Moses' conversation with God (Exodus 20. 18–21).

My favourite angel passage concerns Elijah's successor, Elisha. The King of Aram was incensed that his plans for attacking the Israelite army always seemed to be known beforehand by the enemy. The blame was set squarely on the prophet Elisha, whose clairvoyant gifts allowed him to warn the King of Israel in advance about the Aramaean plans; and so the King of Aram ordered a detachment of his troops to seize Elisha by surrounding the town where he was staying, which was called Dothan. The next morning, Elisha's attendant saw that they were surrounded by a strong force of Aramaean soldiers, and he was terrified. He asked where they were to turn. Elisha offered this prayer: 'Lord, open his eyes and let him see.' The Lord opened the young man's eyes, and he was able to fathom Elisha's assurance that there were more on their side than on the enemy's, for he saw the hills covered with horses and chariots of fire all round Elisha. This is a marvellous demonstration of the ministry of angels protecting those who do God's will in service to their fellow creatures. In this account, Elisha prayed that the enemy force might be struck blind, after which he led them into Samaria, the Israelite capital, when their sight was restored. The account ends on a note of magnanimity; the

Aramaeans are treated to a great feast and then sent back home. There was a cessation of Aramaean raids on Israel for some time afterwards (2 Kings 6.8–23).

In the great writing prophets, angelic intervention is described on only a few occasions. The first is Isaiah's vision of God in the Temple of Jerusalem (Isaiah 6.1–8), which has been alluded to in Chapter 1; seraphim were in attendance on the Lord, and each had six wings, one pair of which covered their faces, another pair their bodies, and the last pair were used for flying. They were calling one to another, 'Holy, holy, holy is the Lord of Hosts: the whole earth is full of his glory.' Isaiah was acutely aware of his uncleanness, and one of the seraphim touched his mouth with a glowing coal taken from the altar with a pair of tongs. This contact served to remove his sinfulness, so that he was able to respond to God's call to service: 'Here am I! Send me' (Isaiah 6.9).

Angelic interpreters are a feature of the later prophetic literature, the earliest being encountered in Ezekiel 40.3–4: 'I saw a man like a figure of bronze standing at the gate and holding a cord of linen thread and a measuring rod. "O man," he said to me, "look closely and listen carefully; note well all that I show you, for this is why you have been brought here. Tell the Israelites everything you see."' The man described here is clearly an angel.

Another prophetic writing that gives prominence to angelic intervention is the Book of Daniel. Although the story takes place during the Babylonian exile, it is generally agreed among scholars that the book was written during the Maccabaean revolt against the hellenizing tyrant Antiochus Epiphanes some four hundred years later (about 165 BC). In the account of the burning fiery furnace, King Nebuchadnezzar decrees that anyone who fails to worship an image he has set up will be cast into the furnace. Three Jewish exiles who are faithful to their own religion refuse to do homage to an image, and trust in God Almighty alone. They are cast into the furnace, but to the amazement of everyone they are seen unharmed in the depth of the furnace together with a fourth person, a man who looks like God. They are released intact, and the king blesses their God who has sent his angel to save his servants. Their trust in him allowed them to disobey the royal command with impunity (Daniel 3, with special reference to verses 24–8). A similar type of event is described in chapter 6 of Daniel: whoever offers a petition to anyone other than the Persian King Darius over the next thirty days is to be cast into the lion-pit. Daniel, chief of the Jewish exiles, continues to make petition to God and is duly apprehended by his jealous enemies. Despite the king's distress, the sentence is executed, but the next morning Daniel is found to be unharmed. He tells the king that God sent his angel to shut the lions' mouths and they had not injured him. God had judged him innocent; and, moreover, he had done the king no injury (Daniel 6.16–22).

The last five chapters of the Book of Daniel have a different emphasis: they deal with things that are to happen in the last days (the study called eschatology). The Book of Daniel names two angels of high degree, usually classed as archangels – though not specifically designated as such in the Bible; these are Gabriel and Michael:

> All the while that I, Daniel, was seeing the vision, I was trying to understand it. Suddenly I saw standing before me one with the appearance of a man; at the same time I heard a human voice calling to him across the bend of the Ulai [a canal mentioned in Daniel 8.2], 'Gabriel, explain the vision to this man.' He came to where I was standing; and at his approach I prostrated myself in terror (Daniel 8.15–17).

Gabriel explains to the terrified Daniel the import of his visions regarding what is to happen at the end of the period of wrath. Gabriel appears again in Daniel 9.21–2, in order to enlighten the prophet's understanding about the things that are to occur in the distant future.

Michael is the guardian angel of the children of God, the Jews; and so we read, '... the guardian angel of the kingdom of Persia [probably a very powerful angel] resisted me for twenty-one days, and then, seeing that I had held out there, Michael, one of the chief princes, came to help me against the prince of the kingdom of Persia' (Daniel 10.13). These are their own guardian angels: 'I have no ally on my side for support and help, except Michael your prince' (Daniel 10.21). In the last chapter, there is an enormous cataclysmic vision that begins:

> At that time there will appear Michael the great captain, who stands guarding your fellow-countrymen; and there will be a period of anguish such as has never been known ever since they became a nation till that moment. But at that time your people will be delivered, everyone whose name is entered in the book: many of those who sleep in the dust will awake, some to everlasting life and some to the reproach of eternal abhorrence (Daniel 12.1–2).

This last verse is the first assurance in the Bible of personal survival of bodily death.

The Book of Zechariah was probably written soon after the return of the Jews to Palestine from Babylonian exile. The prophet is confronted by a series of eight visions that are described in the first five chapters and the first half of the sixth chapter. Each vision is interpreted by an angel close to the prophet. A good example is the eighth vision:

> I looked up again and saw four chariots coming out between two mountains, which were mountains of copper. The first chariot had bay horses, the second black, the third white, and the fourth dappled. I asked the angel who talked with me, 'Sir, what are these?' He answered, 'These are the four winds of heaven; after attending the Lord of the whole earth, they are now going forth. The chariot with the black horses is going to the land of the north, that with the white to the far west, that with the dappled to the south, and that with the roan to the land of the east.' They were eager to set off and range over the whole earth. 'Go,' he said, 'range over the earth,' and they did so. Then he called me to look and said, 'Those going to the land of the north have made my spirit rest on that land' (Zechariah 6.1–8).

It should be recalled that all the major invasions of the Holy

Land (from the Assyrians and Babylonians) had come from the north.

The collection of writings that comprise the Apocrypha contain two significant angelic references. Most of these books, apart from Esdras I and 2 and the Prayer of Manasseh, are included by the Roman Catholic Church as part of the Old Testament. On the other hand, they form no part of the Hebrew scriptures, and the various Reformed Churches separate them into a special collection apart from the remainder of the Old Testament. Here the two Books of Esdras (the Greek Ezra) and Manasseh's Prayer are included. In the delightful story of Tobit, written about 400 BC, Tobit, who has been rendered blind by the warm droppings of sparrows falling into his unprotected eyes (Tobit 2.9–10), ultimately has his sight restored by his son blowing fish-gall into his eyes (Tobit 11.11–15). The instructor in this early medical treatment is the angel Raphael, who also accompanies Tobias, the son, on his difficult journey to Ecbatana in Media. The angel first appears quite unobtrusively as a guide on the way: 'Tobias went out to look for someone who knew the way and would accompany him to Media, and found himself face to face with the angel Raphael. Not knowing he was an angel of God, he questioned him: "Where do you come from, young man?" "I am an Israelite," he replied, "one of your fellow-countrymen, and I have come here to find work" (Tobit 5.4–5). Together they go to Media where Tobias is able to marry Sarah, the daughter of his kinsfolk Raguel and Edna. Until then, all Sarah's prospective marriages had been foiled by the demon Asmodaeus. Before the intervention of Raphael, both Tobit and Sarah had longed for death, hence Raphael is always regarded as the angel associated with healing.

In Christian usage there are three archangels: Michael (which means Who-is-like-God?), Gabriel (which means God is my strength), and Raphael (which means God heals). The Jews have a fourth angel, Uriel (which means God is my light). He is one of the seven holy angels (see below) over the world and over Tartarus, as recounted in the apocryphal Book of Enoch 20.2. It is said that the Lord set him over all the luminaries in heaven; in this capacity he served as guide for Enoch in his imaginary journeys through heaven and the underworld. Uriel is also the angel who instructs Salathiel (Ezra), in 2 Esdras 4.1 (probably written in the first century AD), about the mysteries of the universe. The Jews have a special blessing in which all four archangels are invoked in prayer. Apart from this quartet, no other angels in the Bible are given special names. Among ecstatic Jews in the later centuries, apocryphal writings abound that name a host of angels, an extravagent miscellany that seem to be individually in control of many natural phenomena. This type of angelology has done the subject considerable harm, since modern science can explain such phenomena much more convincingly in terms of well-defined laws. I would never be so bold as to exclude angelic influence from any sphere of cosmic activity, but I would expect it to act coherently as part of the divine initiative rather than as idiosyncratic exhibitions of purpose. Raphael himself is presented as one of the seven angels who stand in attendance on the Lord and enter his glorious presence (Tobit 12.15). The list of the seven angels has been extravagantly completed by apocryphal writers. One also recalls the seven angels of the Apocalypse described in Revelation 8.2, and that we mention in Chapter 3.

The Psalms contain a number of references to angels. The best known is Psalm 91.10–12: 'You have made the Most High your dwelling-place; no disaster will befall you, no calamity touch your home. For he will charge his angels to guard you wherever you go, to lift you on their hands.' This passage was quoted by the devil when he tempted Jesus in the wilderness (Matthew 4.5–7). Some other Psalm quotations concerning angels are: 'The angel of the Lord is on guard round those who fear him, and he rescues them' (Psalm 34.7); 'May they be like chaff before the wind, driven away by the angel of the Lord!' (Psalm 35.5); 'There were myriads of God's chariots, thousands upon thousands, when the Lord came in holiness from Sinai' (Psalm 68.17, which refers to Elisha and the chariots of fire that he revealed to his terrified servant at Dothan); 'So everyone ate the bread of angels; he sent them food in plenty' (Psalm 78.25); 'He unleashed his blazing anger on them, wrath and enmity and rage, launching those messengers of evil' (Psalm 78.49, which refers to the demonic spirits that act as destroying angels); 'Bless the Lord, you his angels, mighty in power, who do his bidding and obey his command' (Psalm 103.20); 'Praise him, all his angels; praise him, all his hosts' (Psalm 148.2).

It is evident from these various accounts that the angels are creatures distinct from God, but members of the heavenly court, where they are called 'sons of God', 'holy ones', and 'host of heaven'. Good passages to illustrate this are: 'Micaiah went on, "Listen now to the word of the Lord: I saw the Lord seated on his throne, with all the host of heaven in attendance on his right and on his left"' (1 Kings 22.19); Psalm 148.2 (quoted above); and 'You alone are the Lord; you created the heavens, the highest heavens with all their host, the earth and all that is on it, the seas and all that is in them. You give life to them all, and the heavenly host worships you' (Nehemiah 9.6). Job 1.6–12 and 2.1–6 evoke the angelic gathering from which God sends his messengers, or angels, down to earth. Some are destructive in character, others have a guardian function, while yet others have an intermediary function in prophecy. Some of this has already been witnessed.

Thus it is clear that the Old Testament is a hive of angelic activity, and its ramifications are continued in the New Testament, as we will now see in Chapter 3.

3

Angels in the New Testament

◆◆◆

Angelic visitations are prominent at the extremes of Jesus' life — at the time of his birth, and during the period of his death and resurrection. The Gospels of Matthew and Luke describe his birth from the points of view of Joseph and Mary respectively. In Matthew's account, Mary was found to be pregnant before her marriage, and Joseph, a kindly man, was all set on dissolving the betrothal as quietly as possible to save his intended spouse from any scandal — betrothal being a state of being bound to another with a promise of marriage. However, an angel of God appeared to Joseph in a dream, assuring him that all was well, and that he should not flinch from accepting Mary as his lawful wife. It is of interest that the angel made itself and its message known while Joseph was asleep. The message proved authentic; and later, after the fleeing of the holy family to Egypt in order to escape King Herod's murderous intent, it was once more an angel of God who summoned them back to the land of Israel, where they eventually settled in Nazareth. Dreams play a part in deciding Joseph's journey, but an angel is not mentioned again (all this is described in chapter 2 of Matthew's Gospel).

In Luke's account, the story begins with Elizabeth and her husband, the priest Zechariah; as in a number of other biblical narratives, this couple were childless and getting on in years. Then suddenly, the archangel Gabriel appeared to Zechariah during his term of duty in the temple, and forecast that a son to be called John was soon to be born to them. In the sixth month of Elizabeth's pregnancy, Gabriel also visited the much younger Mary, who was betrothed to Joseph and still a virgin. She was told that she would conceive and give birth to a son, whom she was to name Jesus; he would be great and called Son of the Most High. When she protested that she was still a virgin, the angel told her that the Holy Spirit would come upon her and the power of the Most High overshadow her; for this reason, the holy child to be born would be called Son of God. When her kinswoman Elizabeth's pregnancy was also revealed to Mary by the angel, she hurried at once to Elizabeth's home to greet her joyfully. We are told that Elizabeth's six-month-old foetus at once stirred in her womb, a memorable illustration of the way in which the Holy Spirit operates in our lives, stirring us up for some action.

All this and much more is recounted in the first chapter of Luke's Gospel, while in the second chapter, the birth narrative of Jesus is recorded. An angel of the Lord appeared to some shepherds, and the glory of the Lord shone round them. The shepherds were terrified, but the angel told them not to be afraid, for he brought good news: the Messiah had been born. The sign would be a baby wrapped in swaddling clothes, lying in a manger. All at once there was with the angel a great company of the heavenly host, singing praise to God: 'Glory to God in highest heaven, and on earth peace to all in whom he delights.' After the angels had left them and returned to heaven, the shepherds went straight to Bethlehem to see what had happened. The especially interesting feature of this chapter is the limited part played by the angels in the narrative, compared with the decidedly more important presence of the Holy Spirit who inspired a number of people to ecstatic prophetic utterance. It was, however, the angel that gave the name 'Jesus' to Mary's baby before his conception (Luke 2.21).

At the end of Jesus' life, the angels once more make their appearance. During the ordeal attending the mighty conflict with the forces of evil that dominated the events witnessed at Gethsemane, an angel came from heaven to give Jesus strength (Luke 22.43), while Jesus in the anguish of spirit prayed the more urgently. In John's account of Jesus' anguish, a kind of parallel to the Gethsemane episode recorded in the Synoptic Gospels, the crowd standing by heard a voice from heaven that sounded both like thunder and the voice of an angel (John 12.29). Jesus told them that this voice spoke for their benefit, not his. The hour of the world's judgement had arrived, and the prince of the world would be driven out. It must be admitted that this prince, who is the devil, is still very much with us, but I believe a higher wisdom to be at work, as I shall discuss in Chapter 7.

Much earlier on in Jesus' ministry, at the end of the temptations in the wilderness where he had been led quite deliberately by the Holy Spirit to be tempted by the devil, after he had successfully resisted the diabolical challenge to self-glorification, the devil departed for the time being, and angels came and attended to his needs (Matthew 4.11). Thus there was clearly a close relationship between Jesus and the angelic hierarchy.

After the crucifixion and subsequent burial, an angel of the Lord descended from heaven and rolled away the stone from the tomb's entrance, then sat on it. This angel showed its typical appearance: face shining like lightning and garments white as snow. Its appearance filled the guards with dread, but to the women standing there (Mary of Magdala and Mary the mother of James and Joseph), it said, 'You ... have nothing to fear. I know you are looking for Jesus who was crucified. He is not here; he has been raised, as he said he would be. Come and see the place where he was laid, and then go quickly and tell his disciples: "He has been raised from the dead and is going ahead of you into Galilee; there you will see him." That is what I came to tell you' (Matthew 28.5–7). A relatively similar report is described in Mark 16.4–7 and Luke 24.2–7.

In John's account, Mary of Magdala was first to discover the empty tomb, and she ran to tell Peter and John, who were amazed to confirm that it was so, and then returned home. Mary remained disconsolately:

And as she wept, she peered into the tomb, and saw two angels in white sitting there, one at the head, and one at the feet, where the body of Jesus had lain. They asked her, 'Why are you weeping?' She answered, 'They have taken my Lord away, and I do not know where they have laid him.' With these words she turned round and saw Jesus standing there, but she did not recognize him (John 20.11–14).

The last account of angels in Jesus' life story occurs at the time of the Ascension. When all the apostles (apart from Judas Iscariot) were together, he parried their simplistic questions about restoring sovereignty to Israel, but promised them rather mysteriously the advent of their baptism into the Holy Spirit. Then he was lifted up before their very eyes. While they were gazing into the sky as he went, all at once there stood beside them two men robed in white. These angels told them to stop looking up at the sky: Jesus, who had been taken from them up to heaven, would come in the same way as they had seen him go (Acts 1.6–9).

Jesus mentioned angels on a number of occasions in his teaching. In the parable of the darnel (translated 'tares' in the Authorized Version) told in Matthew 13.24–30, Jesus identifies the reapers with angels; the Son of Man will send his angels, who will gather out of his Kingdom every cause of sin, and all those whose deeds are evil, all of which will be thrown into the burning furnace (Matthew 13.41–3). This image may offend because of its irreversibility, but the call for immediate repentance is not to be lightly dismissed. In Matthew 18.10 we encounter a milder, but no less radical, teaching: 'See that you do not despise one of these little ones; I tell you, they have their angels in heaven, who look continually on the face of my heavenly Father.' These are the guardian angels whom we all have; while the intellectually sophisticated are far too entranced with their own knowledge to accommodate any awareness of a power outside themselves that guards them and brings them everlastingly to the divine light, the simple ones of this world, who include children, are in much closer contact with spiritual reality. I believe that every living form has an angelic guide and protector; we shall think about this again in Chapter 4.

In Matthew 24.36, in the final part of the great eschatological discourse (on the last things before the the coming of the Son in glory, which is called the parousia), Jesus reminded them all that no one knows the exact time of the coming, not even the angels in heaven (who have very close access to God). In the fine eschatological parable of Matthew 25.31–46, the parable of the sheep and the goats – which is also the parable of the

Last Judgement — Jesus envisaged the Son of Man coming in all his glory and all the angels with him, sitting on his glorious throne with all the nations gathered before him. At Jesus' betrayal, when a supporter cut off the ear of the high priest's servant, Jesus immediately told him to put away his sword. Did he not suppose that his Father would send him twelve legions of angels if he appealed to him (Matthew 26.51–3)?

In Mark's Gospel we find two additional allusions to angels. 'If anyone is ashamed of me and my words in this wicked and godless age, the Son of Man will be ashamed of him, when he comes in the glory of his Father with the holy angels' (Mark 8.38). The other one is as follows: 'When they rise from the dead, men and women do not marry; they are like angels in heaven' (Mark 12.25). This remark was said in reply to the Sadducees, who maintained that there was no resurrection (since it was not found in the teaching of Moses). A rather similar reply is found in Luke 20.34–6: 'Jesus said to them, "The men and women of this world marry; but those who have been judged worthy of a place in the other world, and of the resurrection from the dead, do not marry, for they are no longer subject to death. They are like angels; they are children of God, because they share in the resurrection."' It is worthy of comment that the resurrected dead are not actually angelic, but merely resemble angels in their proximity to God. Unlike the angels, they have much work of character-building to perform; this development of the full person by the process of growth is the special task set before humans, and it is the essential way towards glorification in the pattern of the supreme divine person, Jesus Christ.

In the parable of the rich man (often called Dives) and Lazarus (Luke 16.19–31), it is angels who carry away the soul of Lazarus to be with Abraham. This parable is exceptional in Luke's collection for the unremittingly harsh treatment meted out to the selfish plutocrat, now in hell. Not even a return of Lazarus from the dead will redeem his five brothers from their fate, because Moses and the prophets have said it all; if they remain impervious to the teachings of these men, they will never be converted — even by a visitor from the country of the dead. One might add in parentheses that a certain Saul of Tarsus was well-schooled in the Scriptures, yet persisted in persecuting the earliest Christians until someone from the dead did indeed address him and set him on the right way. It goes to show how unwise it is ever to be dogmatic about anything in this world; rather we should try to help our fellow creatures no matter how far astray they appear to be in the life they lead. The evil apparent in many of us is as much a reflection of the society in which we live as our own unworthiness; if we were open to the bright angels around us, we would go astray much less often.

The mention of angels is prominent in the Acts of the Apostles. In the interrogation and address of defence of the proto-martyr Stephen, all who were sitting in the Council fixed their eyes on him, and his face seemed to them like the face of an angel (Acts 6.25). In his defence in Acts 7.35, Stephen asserted that God spoke to Moses through an angel who appeared to him in the burning bush, while in Acts 7.53 he said that the Jews received the Law given by God's angels and yet had not kept it. In a concurrent passage a little earlier in this discourse, Stephen said, 'It was he [Moses] who, in the assembly in the desert, kept company with the angel, who spoke to him on Mount Sinai, and with our forefathers, and received the living utterances of God to pass on to us' (Acts 7.38). As we have previously noted, the 'angel of God' is, in the earliest writings, identical with God manifesting himself. Later on, a distinction was made between God and his angel in order to emphasize the divine transcendence. And so it comes about that Moses was not in direct communication with God, but with one or several angels.

Angels play an important part in the conversion of the first Gentile to the Christian faith (Acts 10). Cornelius, the centurion in the Italian Cohort and a great friend of the Jewish religion, was summoned to send to Joppa for Peter by direct angelic orders. He thereupon sent three of his personnel to Joppa, during which time Peter was being prepared spiritually for their arrival: he had a shattering vision in which he was taught that he should not consider anything God had made to be unclean.

When the party arrived at Peter's door, the full import of the vision became clear to him: Cornelius, a devout man and a great sympathizer of Judaism, was now ready for reception into the Christian community. Peter invited the party into his lodging for the night, and the next day they all left Joppa and travelled to Caesarea, where Cornelius greeted Peter with great humility. Whereas Peter would previously have demurred from even sharing a meal with the gentile Cornelius (and the others), he now had no compunction in baptizing them all. That the decision was right was proved by the outpouring of the Holy Spirit on them while Peter was still speaking, before the baptism itself. In this instance we see an interesting collaboration between the angels and the Holy Spirit: the angels do the preparatory work for the baptism, while the effulgence of the Holy Spirit embraces the men as they are about to enter fully into the Christian faith.

Angelic power was demonstrated in the miraculous release of Peter from prison, where he had been confined by the vindictive King Herod, fresh from beheading James, the brother of John. While Peter was languishing in prison and the whole community prayed for him, an angel of God appeared so that the cell was ablaze with light. The angel released him and opened all the prison doors, so that when he appeared at the door of Mary's house (the mother of John Mark), the maid-servant Rhoda was so overcome with amazement that she left Peter at the door and announced his presence to the party inside the house. He went on knocking until he was finally admitted, when he recounted his amazing story (Acts 12.4–17). Herod commanded the interrogation and execution of all the prison guards.

Angels are also mentioned in Acts 23.8–9 in respect of a dispute between Sadducees and Pharisees concerning the possible angelic interpretation of St Paul's vision on the road to Damascus, but confusion rather than light followed the futile debate. The final mention of angels is recorded in Acts 27.23, in which Paul recorded a vision of an angel of God who proceeded to tell him not to be afraid: it was ordained that Paul should appear before Caesar, and that he could rejoice in the fact that God had granted him the lives of all who were sailing with him.

The letters of Paul bear only scant reference to angels, sometimes with a distinctly pejorative odour. Good examples of this are: 'Satan himself masquerades as an angel of light' (2 Corinthians 11.14); 'But should anyone, even I myself or an angel from heaven, preach a gospel other than the gospel I preached to you, let him be banned' (Galatians 1.8); 'For I am convinced that there is nothing in death or life, in the realm of spirits or superhuman powers ... that can separate us from the love of God in Christ Jesus our Lord' (Romans 8.38–9); 'Are you not aware that we are to judge angels, not to mention day by day affairs' (I Corinthians 6.3); 'Though I speak in tongues of men or of angels, but if I have no love, I am a sounding gong or a clanging cymbal' (I Corinthians 13.1); 'You are not to be disqualified by the decision of people who go in for self-mortification and angel-worship and access to some visionary world' (Colossians 2.18). More encouraging texts are: 'It is just that God should balance the account by sending affliction to those who afflict you, and relief to you who are afflicted, and to us as well, when the Lord Jesus is revealed from heaven with his mighty angels in blazing fire' (2 Thessalonians 1.6–8); 'And great beyond all question is the mystery of our religion: He was manifested in flesh, vindicated in spirit, seen by angels; he was proclaimed among the nations, believed in throughout the world, raised to heavenly glory' (I Timothy 3.16). A Letter to Hebrews, of unknown authorship, has informative comments about angels: '[The Son] is raised as far above the angels as the title he has inherited is superior to theirs' (1.4), which is followed by a comparison that fills the remainder of the first chapter; 'For if God's word spoken through angels had such force ...' (2.2); 'For it is not to angels that he has subjected the world to come ...' (2.5); 'Clearly they are not angels whom he helps, but the descendants of Abraham' (2.16); 'No, you have come to Mount Zion, the city of the living God, the heavenly Jerusalem, to myriads of angels' (12.22); 'Do not neglect to show hospitality; by doing this, some have entertained angels unawares' (13.2).

The First Letter of Peter contains two useful comments

about angels: 'These are things that angels long to glimpse' (1.12); 'Who [Jesus] is now at the right hand of God, having entered heaven and received the submission of angels, authorities, and powers' (3.22). The Second Letter of Peter also contains two allusions to angels: 'God did not spare the angels who sinned, but consigned them to the dark pits of hell, where they are held for judgement' (2.4); '... whereas angels, for all their superior strength and power, employ no insults in seeking judgement against them [lascivious humans] before the Lord' (2.11). The Letter of Jude contains a relevant reference: 'Remember too those angels who were not content to maintain the dominion consigned to them, but abandoned their proper dwelling-place; God is holding them, bound in darkness with everlasting chains, for judgement on the great day' (verse 6). This intriguing argument depends on certain apocryphal Jewish writings. According to the Book of Enoch, the angels let themselves be seduced by the 'daughters of men', as recounted in Genesis 6.1–4. In verse 9, the archangel Michael is mentioned simply to compare his mild expostulation with the devil in the matter of the possession of Moses' body with the abuse hurled by certain heretics who were troubling the young Church. The incident referred to appears to originate in another apocryphal text, the Assumption of Moses.

In the Book of Revelation (of John), a more extensive counterpart of the Book of Daniel in the Old Testament, angels find their most striking role. John – almost certainly not the writer of the fourth Gospel, but probably a member of his circle of disciples – was imprisoned on the island of Patmos because of his Christian allegiance. There he had a profound spiritual experience in which the Holy Spirit revealed the risen Lord to him, who was commanded to write down all he saw and was shown about the future. Like the Book of Daniel, Revelation is primarily a message of hope for a group of believers severely ravaged by vicious adversaries who seemed to be succeeding without any restraint. First came a message of instruction and admonition to the seven churches of the Province of Asia (on the west coast of modern Turkey) at Ephesus, Smyrna, Pergamum, Thyatira, Sardis, Philadelphia and Laodicea, and the message was addressed to the angel of the respective church. After this, the scene changed to visions of heaven: God was sitting on the throne, surrounded by twenty-four elders seated on their thrones. In God's hand there was a scroll sealed with seven seals. Then a powerful angel cried with a loud voice, 'Who is worthy to break the seals and open the scroll?' (5.2). It was the Lamb who was alone eligible to receive the scroll, to the worship of the vast multitude which included the voices of many angels, thousands on thousands, myriads on myriads. There was the collective proclamation, 'Worthy is the Lamb who was slain, to receive power and wealth, wisdom and might, honour and glory and praise!' (5.11–12); and so God entrusted the future of the world to the Lamb.

When the seals were broken, the great punishment in store for the world was forecast, together with the consolation of the martyrs waiting for justice to be done in their cause. Chapter 7 describes four angels given the power to devastate the wicked earth, so that only the chosen few who were specially sealed on their foreheads were exempt from punishment. There then appeared a great multitude of risen martyrs robed in white and holding palm branches. All the angels who stood around the throne prostrated themselves before it and worshipped God, crying, 'Amen! Praise and glory and wisdom, thanksgiving and honour, power and might, be to our God for ever! Amen' (7.12). As the vision proceeded, the seven angels were each given a trumpet (8.2); and when these were blown, various cosmic disasters occurred. Chapter 12 is of great importance in describing the fall of Satan from heaven to the earth: 'Then war broke out in heaven; Michael and his angels fought against the dragon. The dragon with his angels fought back, but he was too weak, and they lost their place in heaven. The great dragon was thrown down, that ancient serpent who led the whole world astray, whose name is the Devil, or Satan; he was thrown down to the earth, and his angels with him' (12.7–9).

In chapter 14 of Revelation the angels announce the advent of the Day of Judgement, while in chapter 16 the seven angels pour out the seven bowls of God's wrath upon the earth. In the following two chapters, the angels celebrate the fall of

Babylon, which is usually identified with Rome. Then follows a magnificent vision of the marriage of the Lamb: 'The angel said to me, "Write this: 'Happy are those who are invited to the wedding banquet of the Lamb!'" He added, "These are the very words of God." I prostrated myself to worship him, but he said, "You must not do that! I am a fellow-servant with you and your brothers who bear their witness to Jesus. It is God you must worship. For those who bear witness to Jesus have the spirit of prophecy"' (19.9–10). In the concluding chapters of this magnificent, often repetitive, confusing, and thoroughly inspiring book, the angels play a decisive part in the destruction of the devil from the earth, as the Day of Judgement draws near for all people to be assessed according to how they have lived on earth and the nature of their deeds. 'Then the angel showed me the river of the water of life, sparkling like crystal, flowing from the throne of God and of the Lamb down the middle of the city's street. On either side of the river stood a tree of life, which yields twelve crops of fruit, one for each month of the year. The leaves of the trees are for the healing of the nations' (22.1–2). How great a part the angelic hierarchy play in this great vision of hope in the ultimate triumph of good over evil that characterizes the whole of John's revelation!

I have compiled this list of angelic appearances in the Bible not in a spirit of pious literalism, usually called fundamentalism, but simply to show how extraterrestrial information and help have come to the aid of people, and have also been a means of instruction to leaders and prophets. Some accounts certainly have a legendary ring to them, but those appertaining to prophecy have, in my estimation, an immediacy that I associate with truth. In the angelology of the later prophets Ezekiel, Zechariah, and Daniel, in which the angels interpret the vision of the prophet, I feel most at home. There is a veracity that speaks to my inner condition, and leads me forward in my own endeavours. By contrast, the various birth stories in both Testaments have a mythological flavour. This does not diminish their basic validity, so much as suggest that angels are being used as symbols to illustrate the inexplicable. Religion transcends the purely rational, hence it cannot be confined to rational categories. It extends our understanding through mystical encounter, which in turn may broaden our view of the process of life. True religion leads to a spiritual unfolding that culminates in the vision of God, whereas false religion usurps the function of God in its own institutions.

It is of interest that early on in the world's history of angels, a number of categories appeared: choirs of singers, a military presence (the Elisha apparition that rings profoundly true to my imagination), members of the heavenly court (as in the first two chapters of the Book of Job), guardians, helpers, sustainers, protectors, and judges. Nowadays angels are present in the popular imagination in one predominant category, portrayed classically as the winged cherub that clearly functions as a messenger. But in fact all these apparently distinct groups have a common gift endowed by God: they all in one way or another transmit his uncreated light to his many creatures, whether in body, mind, or soul. The light opens the mind to truth and the heart to compassion of a degree seen in the ministry of Jesus. The body begins to radiate a health that may affect many others in its vicinity.

I believe that we are encompassed in a blanket of angelic activity. In the course of daily life, we (apart from a few profoundly mystical people) are closed to the presence of angels (except perhaps in a great crisis), for we tend to be very easily distracted by worldly matters. An open heart and a generous attitude to life are features that make us especially amenable to angelic communication; the closed mind and stony heart resist the ingress of angelic activity. It is hardly surprising that academic theologians and scientific workers have great difficulty with the concept of angels.

It must be conceded that in the Middle Ages the angels were credited with such functions as the movement of the stars and the activity of the universe. St Paul writes of this in Ephesians 6.12: 'For our struggle is not against human foes, but against cosmic powers, against the authorities and potentates of this dark age, against the superhuman forces of evil in the heavenly realms.' In our scientifically oriented world, the movement of the planets and much else in our vast universe is quite satisfactorily explained in terms of natural function. It

4
The Experience of Angels

❖❖❖

What is it like to experience an angel? The appearance, or lack of appearance, varies, but one knows immediately that one is in communication with something very unusual. Apart from the dream-vision with which I begin this book, my own encounters with angels have been non-material – indeed, exceptionally spiritual. This is extremely biblical: 'He makes his angels winds, and his ministers flames of fire' (Hebrews 1.7). I know my angel, surely my guardian angel in whom I believe absolutely, by his insistent voice in my life. Whenever I have done anything clearly wrong in my relationship with someone else, my angel has made me aware of my misdemeanour in no uncertain way. His insistence that I put matters right, and as soon as possible, cannot be evaded. The things I have done wrong have not been major offences, but instead the tendency to be irritable and impatient with someone who was clearly seeking my assistance.

On one occasion much earlier in my life, a colleague insisted that I should play my part at work. My refusal was a response to imagined injustice, not to the burden of work itself, a 'burden' I have always enjoyed. Injustice, though, was another matter, especially as the colleague was of equal status to me, and in no position to make demands. The outcome was that I was cold-shouldered, and the isolation became intolerable. At that point, the angel spoke to me interiorly and reasoned with me. He told me to make my peace with the colleague rather than continue a state of affairs that could have progressed to a smouldering feud. I would, of course, have to humble myself before him and apologize, but the urge was so strong that I obeyed forthwith, and at once harmony was restored. The angel gave me the strength to humiliate myself, so that I could apologize without emotional pain. The matter was clearly trifling, but the mechanism was revealing. It was my conscience that made me seek a rapprochement in a very trivial affair, and this conscience has been my guide throughout my life. Though I am not a particularly guilt-ridden person, when one is traversing the spiritual path even small irregularities may cause one to stumble. This is the price one pays for spiritual progress. What might cause 'the man in the street' to shrug his shoulders in complete unconcern is of discomfort to a person of spiritual awareness. By 'spiritual' I mean appertaining to God, and some people are aware of this quest and purpose to their lives at an extremely early age.

When I am brusque with troublesome people on the telephone, my guardian angel helps to keep my temper cool, so that I am not in danger of exploding. All this sounds very unspiritual indeed, but if one is confronted by a veritable mountain of work, the irritability, though an undoubted failure which should not be indulgently dismissed, may become slightly more understandable – and to understand all is to become increasingly tolerant. The end of all this naked display of impatience is to attain that very understanding: 'To be patient shows great understanding; quick temper is the height of folly' (Proverbs 14.29). I feel I have attained a little of this understanding over the years, but my relapses when I sense injustice show me that a long way still has to be travelled. What I am saying is this: the directive force of conscience is one's guardian angel. My guardian angel also protects me from narrow scrapes when driving, and when walking on dangerous terrain. So often our minds are concerned with other matters when performing these routine actions, but the angel can get through in an emergency and save the day. I never forget to thank God for his providential care, and to salute the angel as a true friend. It is, however, necessary to add that none of us is exempt from tragedies of one type or another. In Chapter 7 I consider the part that the dark angels play in our personal, and even spiritual, growth. Nevertheless, even in the midst of a terrible accident our guardian angel can strengthen us, giving us the courage to bear all subsequent suffering.

In my deliverance work, it is my angel who provides me with the essential way of approach. I only do this work when in a state of rapt prayer, in which I believe I am in close spiritual union with the Holy Trinity. I ask the question, and my angel gives me the answer. (I discuss the matter fully in Chapter 6 in connection with angels of darkness.) It is God who provides the answer, but the angel is used to indicate the way ahead. Much as I value the presence of my guardian angel, I do not pray to him. My devotions are to God the Holy Trinity, Father, Son, and Holy Spirit. In deliverance work I include the names God the Creator and God Most High to the trinitarian formula, since some alien spirits appear not to acknowledge the name of the Holy Trinity, whereas they may respond to the name of the Creator. Why this should be I do not know. I do not discountenance those who pray to angels and saints inasmuch as these are ways towards the Godhead, but a person endowed with mystical awareness does not require intermediaries. Yet, remember, mystical awareness brings with it an awareness of the pain of all the world. To whom much is given, much is expected.

When the manifold functions that my guardian angel fulfils in my life are reviewed, especially those involved in the workings of conscience, it could be argued that it is all simply the voice of the Holy Spirit. I broach this topic later in the chapter, but at this point I include two experiences shared with me by a friend, in order to indicate the relatively circumscribed nature of an angelic apparition:

> I was driving up to the Lake District to collect some sheep, towing a trailer, when the trailer destabilized and the car went out of control and charged off the side of the motorway. I was certain I was about to die, but in fact the car ran into a bramble patch, and I stepped out quite unhurt. It took all day to sort out the resulting mess and drive myself home in a hired car, and I arrived back in the country in a thoroughly shaken-up state. I had been feeling very open to God as I drove up, thinking over some particularly beautiful verses of a psalm, and that feeling also stayed with me. I got home just in time for Evensong, which it felt like a good idea to go to. As I knelt down in the church, a remarkable thing started to happen. It's very difficult to put into words, but

one could perhaps describe it as a welling-up of invisible light – a feeling of stillness, calmness, sweetness, radiance, distance, deepness – and a specific limitation both in duration (it seemed like a couple of minutes) and space. The radiance reached all round from the focal point (I suppose one's consciousness), but things nearby were held more strongly in it.

I have a small dog who sometimes gets into a nervous state, and then I just pick him up and hold him until I can feel he's calmed down. I had that sensation then very strongly, that I was simply being picked up and held until my state of nerves went away. The message *wasn't* anything so corny as being personally protected – God might well choose to snuff me out tomorrow in another car crash – but there was something to do with trust, and all being ultimately well.

Here is my friend's second experience:

This was a few months later than the previous occurrence. My daughter had just discovered that she had precancerous changes in her cervix. I was in a state of great misery – not only with a mother's natural worry, but with a deep guilt because I knew that such things were often caused by stress (which lowers the body's resistance), and I was very frightened that I had contributed not only by being a bad mother when she was young, but by my bad behaviour recently which had greatly upset her. I happened to be passing the British Museum with half an hour to spare, so I thought I'd go in and have a good look at the Elgin Marbles. Usually I have the greatest difficulty in actually seeing works of art (or hearing music), no matter how hard I try to look (or listen). There's a barrier between me and the object, and I can't understand it or bring it to life. But this time, as soon as I started to look at the Marbles, the same radiance started to pour out of them, so that each one spoke to me of beauty and truth; and I could comprehend the meaning of every shape, and they filled me with joy, so that I wanted to laugh as I looked at them. This lasted as long as I was in the room where they live, and drained away as I left them, so maybe twenty to thirty minutes, less intense though and more outward-looking than the other time. The message there was again simple — comfort and joy — for life is transient and we are cut down as grass. But none of that matters, because eternity lies all round us and only a veil prevents us seeing it.

Here we have some other properties of angels, channels of light and messengers of purpose and love. My angel is what I also call my inner voice; it instructs me to do something I would far rather not do. A classical example of this (described in my earlier book, *The Quest for Wholeness*[1]) concerned my reactions to my premature retirement from my medical post. I would much rather have sought medical employment elsewhere, a preference endorsed by all my friends, but the inner voice told me to be quiet and to continue seeing people in my flat for healing and counselling. A year later, I was appointed priest-in-charge of the church in which I had been serving in a non-stipendiary, assistant capacity; and so a completely new work confronted me, one that would have been impossible to perform had I taken a medical post elsewhere.

The guardian angel is not an inner teacher, like a well-known Jungian archetype. This is a complex to be found in the unconscious in many different people in widely different periods, part of the psychic structure of the human being. It is well described in *Experiment in Depth* by P.W. Martin.[2] Instead, the guardian angel is a practical director that will not let one alone until one has done the proper thing. I prefer the word 'proper' to the word 'right' in human situations, for we do not know what is right or wrong until the final moral balance-sheet has been set before us after we have experienced bodily death. Yet the 'proper' action sets us on the course whereby we may grow spiritually, a growth that always entails service to our fellow creatures in a way commensurate with our own particular talents. Not infrequently it sets us against the majority, so inculcating courage in us. It should be noted that angels are spiritual beings, so therefore angelic encounters are a type of spiritual experience whose characteristically distinctive feature are their circumscribed, or localized, nature, whether spatial in the outer world or intrapsychic in the conscience.

There is an increasing literature of angelic appearances noted by very ordinary (I speak ironically) people in the course of their daily work. It is not without amusement that as professional theologians find the concept of angels more and more difficult to accept, our good friend 'the man in the street' is seeing things that make him wonder. Unless he consults a sympathetic psychotherapist (a necessary procedure before any angelic apparition can be accepted as valid and not merely a fantasy conjured up by the mind, with its excellent powers of dramatization), there will always remain doubt as to the true nature of what is perceived. People who are mentally ill are sometimes plagued with hallucinations, which are apparent perceptions of external objects not actually present. Since the encounter with an angel is usually a private matter, it could come into the category of an hallucination, but in this case the person is usually mentally sound, so that one can accept their story without too much doubt. A little doubt is not a bad thing until one has had a paranormal encounter oneself. If the encounter with an alleged angel inflates the ego so that one feels that one is a rather special person, one should beware: psychic inflation is not a pleasant state, and requires special treatment from therapists who are knowledgeable about psychic matters.

A frequent visual form of an angel is that of a tall being with a human face, well over six feet tall, which may envelop a person or else stand a little distance away from them. There is a distinctive aura of light around the angel, and it seems to act as a protective presence, particularly when peril is sensed as being afoot. Sometimes there is no personification, but simply a focus of light. Usually there are the characteristic wings so well depicted in medieval and renaissance Christian painting, but these are usually additions that have been conjured up by the mind of the beholder. This brings us to the important point as to whether angels are as they appear to us because they really look like this, or because our minds have translated the formless, non-material nature of an angel into a form that we can recognize and communicate with in confidence. (We shall consider this matter later on in the book.) The pseudo-Dionysius had considerable contempt for the description of the cherubim as winged creatures (we encountered biblical examples in Chapter I), but in the end he sees the value of God's presenting these senior members of the angelic hierarchy in a form easily accessible to ordinary people. The paintings of the great Christian masters of earlier centuries depict angels' great beauty and inspiring human faces, as well as their wings. A far more contemporary painter, Marc Chagall, who delighted in depicting angels, continued this tradition – even if his angels are somewhat less splendid than their renaissance ancestors! It is worth remembering that winged beings and celestial messengers are to be seen in the art of the Sumerians, Babylonians, Egyptians, Greeks, and Romans. The celebrated *Victory of Samothrace*, now in the Louvre in Paris, depicts one of the most wonderful winged figures in existence; though female, it is very like the angels depicted by the Christian Church.

I was somewhat amused recently when a lady who had attended one of my retreats told a friend that she had seen just such a winged angel alongside me as I spoke inspirationally (my way of communication in lecturing, preaching and also writing). I would take this to be the form my guardian angel would assume when visible to a psychically attuned person. Yet even this statement needs qualification. A person like the lady in question would not always see this apparition; it was a gift of grace that brought me and her into spiritual union at that time, and then she was privileged to see what was inaccessible to the other people on the retreat. On another occasion, she might well have seen nothing, *especially* if she had strained every fibre of her being to do so. The winged angelic figure recognized throughout much of the world is a classical Jungian archetype; but, I believe, unlike the usual archetype, is not merely an intrapsychic structure, but has a validity and living power of its own in the world of experience. Now that the experience of non-material, spiritual beings has been recognized by many psychically sensitive people, a typical winged angelic form has fully established itself in the human collective unconscious, which is the outcome of countless generations of humans and their forebears. The winged angelic form has become an important archetype which symbolizes God's providence for all his creatures.

Angels can assume forms other than the classical winged apparition. Among the most convincing are angels that appear as completely human, sometimes as personable young men aiding stranded motorists in appalling weather conditions or helping people in near danger of drowning. Sometimes they avert apparently inevitable traffic accidents. On the other hand, the appearance may be that of an older man who guides strangers to an unknown destination. The essential feature of all these encounters is the sudden appearance of the form, and its equally sudden disappearance once the work has been done. One may look around wanting to thank or pay the helpful stranger, only to find nobody there.

Recently, I had difficulty in starting my new car; a kindly young man came to my help, telling me that the exhaust was discharging a large amount of fumes. He examined the engine and told me that I was flooding it with petrol. He waited a little, and then was able to start the engine. He turned it off, and told me to wait a little before I started it. As he left I offered him payment; he refused and then vanished. Following his advice, I soon got moving to my destination in the country. He seemed pretty full-blooded to me, with strong muscles and firm skin, and I would hesitate to call him a traditional 'angel' – though his origin and whereabouts remained obscure. On the other hand, there were men working in the vicinity, and he could easily have been one of them. What is much more relevant is that he acted as an angel to me, a messenger of God's help, full of concern and active assistance. He may well have had no religious allegiance at all, but I never cease to thank God for his presence in my life and to pray for him. Had he not turned up I should have had to summon professional help, but such a delay would have meant that I would have been late arriving at the religious community I was visiting. (It was very important I arrived punctually because of the tight schedule I had to encompass during my day's stay there.) I often think of Hebrews 13.2, 'Do not neglect to show hospitality; by doing this, some have entertained angels unawares.'

The writer is clearly recalling the visit of God's angels to Abraham, foretelling Isaac's birth and the destruction of the two cities, but the lesson could be of wider application. If only we were more aware of the present moment, many appearances that we normally fail to register in a mind full of negative emotion would make their impact on us and lead us into new fields of discovery. Nearly all recorded accounts of angelic presences occur in crisis situations, either at their peak or shortly afterwards.

In some circumstances, an individual, distraught by long failure, suddenly hears a distinct voice that gives them hope – and sometimes counsel too. Alternatively, the presence of a brilliant light, sometimes in the form of a cross or other religious symbol, brings hope and direction in a situation fraught with doubt and apparent disillusionment. Nearly all these apparitions, including the traditional massive winged figure, are quite personal. Others in the vicinity see nothing, as was the case of the angel close to me in the retreat. The capacity to see angels is not related to the previous spirituality of the person. Often, irreligious people may be privileged to encounter an angelic presence, while a devout believer may be, as it were, left out in the cold. The capacity seems to be a result of the individual's psychic capacity and the grace of God. After all, Christ taught, 'It is not the healthy who need a doctor, but the sick. Go and learn what this text means, "I require mercy, not sacrifice." I did not come to call the virtuous, but sinners' (Matthew 9.12–13). He said this in connection with his habit (much to the disapproval of the Pharisees) of dining with tax-collectors and sinners. In fact, quite a number of non-believers have been converted spontaneously to religion after an angelic encounter. There is indeed much more to existence than the narrow countries that our bigoted minds define, but only a crisis of belief can effect an extension of our horizons.

It may seem unfortunate that most angelic encounters are distinctly personal; if only they could be more widespread! Yet I believe that a misconception lies in this way of thinking. We have to be worthy of any revelation, or else it will simply be part of the common way and no one will value it: 'Do not give dogs what is holy; do not throw your pearls to the pigs: they will only trample on them, and turn and tear you to pieces' (Matthew 7.6). I have little doubt that the commonest, but least spectacular, awareness of angels is an interior psychological release. Someone deep in despair over a real human tragedy suddenly sees the light around what was previously impenetrably dark. It may be an abysmal mistake, a bereavement situation, or even the knowledge that one is suffering from an incurable condition that is shortly to lead to one's death, or else seriously diminish the quality of the remaining years of one's life. One's guardian angel assures one that all is not lost, that he at least is there even if human support is weak and fluctuating. It is then that what was previously unbearable become a challenge, one's inner resources are marshalled, and a new life opens up. A close friend of mine had two angelic encounters some time ago just when she awoke from a good sleep, on both occasions in a convent that she was visiting. On one occasion a presence seemed to embrace her in a friendly way, but on the other she was in a very unhappy state of mind because of a number of personal problems. When she awoke, it was a monk-like figure that greeted her and said quite distinctly that all would be well.

It could be argued that both these encounters were from spirits of the living dead, but they were too diaphanous and fleeting. The 'spirits' (really souls) of the dead tend to be more circumscribed and separate, and show their origin quite clearly, so that one knows the sort of person one is dealing with. Angels, even if they cast a strong form, soon fade into the surrounding atmosphere, and furthermore they bring a spiritual gift of joy, or at least a relief from worry, with them. The living dead are less likely to produce this degree of peace. Admittedly we are on very uneasy ground if we try to pontificate about matters that are accessible to only a relatively few people, but I feel it is important to explore this realm without demur. An angel produces a strong emotional effect, somehow giving information beyond rational explanation. By contrast, the soul of a deceased person tends to give assurance that they are still in some sense alive, and often reveals personal matters of importance to the recipient.

In my experience, visits from the so-called dead have had a definite purpose, giving me advice about such material matters as changing my failing accountant, going to the doctor at once for maladies that I had tended to dismiss as unimportant, and exchanging a large car for a manageable smaller one! My late father has been responsible for these three pieces of counsel. He helped me financially to the best of his ability, remembering that it was possible to transfer only very small amounts of money out of South Africa, where he lived; (he had been a medical practitioner (an eye specialist); and he taught me how to drive some fifty years ago.) Incidentally, it is important to stress that I do not consult mediums; my father's impress is on the mind, quite unprepared as it is for such an encounter. The angel, by contrast, fills me with both aspiration and promised fulfilment on a cosmic level. The result is that I become a more spiritually proficient person (the word 'better' would sound rather priggish, and in fact an angelic visitation produces anything rather than a pious priggishness).

People have on occasion related the unearthly beauty of angelic singing. It is like an enormous choir singing with an harmonic beauty that would appear to be the basis of all music. I myself have heard this celestial harmony, a music that expresses the very heart of beauty; I do not wonder that Plato included beauty with truth and goodness in his triad of ultimate values. To me this harmony is the 'music of the spheres', and a concomitant of mystical illumination. Why should the uncreated light of God that occludes the bodily senses by the very strength of its illumination not have an auditory component also? This would serve to fill the cleansed senses with a fresh draught of ineffable beauty. Whether what I know from experience is identical with the singing of angels I cannot judge; yet there is clearly much in common according to other people's descriptions.

Throughout history, celebrated saints have claimed spiritual intercourse with angels who have directed them on their way. As these encounters are strictly private, one can assess their veracity by their fruits alone. Personally I am always a little wary of people who claim repeated outside angelic encounters, just as I am of those who hear on numerous occasions from deceased friends on the other side of life. My own contact with my father, who shared few of my spiritual interests but was clearly concerned about my well-being after his death, has now ceased, at least on a conscious level. This pleases me, since it indicates that he has more important matters to consider in his new situation, just as I have likewise in my own. Yet my prayer for my parents never slackens, as I would hope is the case with their prayer also. I believe the real angelic contact is an interior one that never ceases. On the contrary, it plays its part in directing our lives along useful channels by which we may gain as much benefit from the present circumstances as possible, while helping others to proceed likewise.

Guardian Angels

The biblical authority for believing that each of us has a guardian angel is Matthew 18.10, 'See that you do not despise one of these little ones; I tell you, they have their angels in heaven, who look continually on the face of my heavenly Father.' These angels therefore live eternally in God's presence, and they bring health to us from the Deity. This belief is especially strong in the Catholic tradition of the Christian Church. As I have previously stated, I have little doubt about the presence of my own guardian angel, whom I regard as the master of the conscience and the divine messenger who inspires me in the work I am called on to do.

Yet where does the Holy Spirit come into all this? One dare not be too dogmatic concerning this matter, but I see the guardian angel as a *servant* of the Spirit, inasmuch as a direct impact with the Spirit might be too shattering in its intensity. We often tend to overlook the function of the ministry of angels and the communion of saints in the vast cosmos. The possibility that every living form is animated by its own particular angelic presence does not offend me; therefore such 'nature spirits' as fairies and gnomes, in which humankind has believed from the very beginning of its creation, are well within the realm of possibility. Nowadays such an hypothesis is laughed to scorn by an unimaginative, sophisticated generation, and indeed such spirits are accessible to only a few psychically sensitive people. In this respect, it is worth noting that even a Jungian archetype has a solid basis on which the image is modelled in the mind. Plato observed that we would not recognize the sun for what it is were there not something sun-like about us, while Pascal remarked that we would not seek God if we had not already found him. Our work is to actualize the interior intuition so as to fulfil our own task and enrich the world.

Another phenomenon, well documented and universally described, in which the guardian angel may possibly reveal itself is in the near-death experience. As a person moves free of the body in a liberated vehicle that can conveniently be called the soul, there is a feeling as if travelling through a dark space, often likened to a tunnel. There is an awareness of a 'presence' that is sensed or inferred, but not directly seen. There is something of a telepathic communication between the individual and the presence, which tends to be related to the decision as to whether to return to earthly life or go on to death. It could be that this presence is the person's guardian angel. If the experience proceeds, the person becomes aware of a brilliant golden light that may envelop them or else draw them into it. The atmosphere is one of great holiness, so that the individual is led to identify the light with God, Christ, Buddha, or some other source of sanctity, depending on the religious tradition they know best. It might also be the guardian angel in another form; at present, of course, we can only speculate.

The angelic hierarchy should not be idolized; this is a constant temptation lying in the path of people of low spirituality and poor education: theirs is the way of superstition. But neither need the angelic forms be superciliously disregarded. Our business is to work close to God; and when we pray, our angel brings us close to the divine source. I personally do not think a great deal about my guardian angel; rather, I see us both intensely involved in the work of intercession that plays so major a part in my prayer life.

Origen wrote, 'All men are moved by two angels, an evil one who inclines them to evil and a good one who inclines them to good ... If there are good thoughts in our hearts, there is no doubt that the angel of the Lord is speaking to us.

But if evil things come into our heart the angel of evil is speaking to us.'[3] We are indeed involved in powerful transpersonal forces, which are bipolar. We may rely on the support of our guardian angels, but we must also be prepared to grapple with our demons. The subject of demonic forces is a difficult but essential matter in any work that considers the angelic powers as something more than merely beneficent forces. For that matter, how much of our character is moulded by personal experience and how much is due to demonic influence? I believe my guardian angel forms the apex of my conscience, but many people seem to have little contact with their conscience, acting without regard for the welfare of others. Presumably the guardian angel is there, but is silent and disregarded. And how does it come to be that the angels who are so close to God can alternatively be members of a destructive community?

It is evident that we need to consider the nature of angels and their actions in further depth if we are to succeed in penetrating their close relationship to the human psyche on the one hand and to God on the other, for they seem quite emphatically to unite the two. The classification of the angelic hierarchy into nine orders that was such a notable achievement of the pseudo-Dionysius deals essentially with the beneficent aspect of angelic activity; but in the considerably more open world of the present time, the approach needs to be more embracing, and the psychological implications cannot be ignored. A penetrating survey of some of the functions and activities of angels can assist us in our quest for a deeper co-operation with them in our own lives, and in the service of the greater world; it is to this that we turn our attention in Chapter 5.

5

The Properties of Angels

◆◆◆

Angels continue to be a popular subject with artists and poets, but theologians seldom have much to say about them – unless the theologians concerned are of fundamentalistic persuasion and accept angels en masse because the Bible repeatedly mentions them. Admittedly, the eucharistic liturgy speaks fulsomely of 'angels and archangels and all the company of heaven' (this is a characteristically Anglican phrase, but the Roman Catholic Mass also mentions the hierarchy in a rather similar context), but the number of priests who really believe in these obscure beings is probably disconcertingly low. Older priests may remember the stories they heard at their mother's knee, and even look back nostalgically to times barely within recall, but younger priests familiar with depth psychology (to say nothing of computer science and its challenge of artificial intelligence) will shake their heads impatiently at the repetition of such nonsense unless personal experience suddenly opens their closed minds to areas of life that were previously hidden from view. This closure of the mind is the result of pride (the attitude that modern humans know it all), ignorance, and a vague, scarcely formulated, fear of the unknown.

So what have modern theologians against angelology – that is, the belief in angels and their scheme in the nature of the universe, and hence in the lives of us all here and now? First, and probably most important, is the allegedly formless, spiritual nature of angelic beings. That which is real should have 'body' – in other words, corporeal substance. The concept of intermediate entities that float around in the cosmos, inaccessible to most of us, becomes unacceptable – especially as developments in cosmology and nuclear physics can explain most of the phenomena of our universe quite satisfactorily. While we are alive, humans function in physical bodies – to the extent

51

that even the Son of God himself became fully human during his salvific work among us, which in a distinctly mystical way continues, and will continue, until the end of the world (at least as far as we poor mortals can glimpse such a profound mystery). The Son of God is with us when we do a charitable act in the course of everyday life, as the solemn parable of the sheep and goats reminds us (Matthew 25.31–46); and when two or three meet together in his name, he is there among them (Matthew 18.20).

The second objection to a belief in angels is closely related to the first. It concerns relying on the help of 'spiritual' agents in such a way as to absolve ourselves from the effort of exercising our own free will. This objection is especially valid when we consider the dark angels, or demonic spirits, and the effect they can have on the human psyche. Again, this matter is a closed book to most people, but no one involved in the work of deliverance, commonly called exorcism, can ignore this question. (We will deal with it later on.) In short, the argument is that a powerful belief in angels can protect us from too close an involvement in the material world in which we are meant to function.

We have already considered the third objection in our mention of nature spirits: too close an attachment to the angelic forces can easily lead to us venerating them. This attitude can lead insidiously to idolatry. There are two passages in the Book of Revelation that explicitly deprecate any such tendency: 'I prostrated myself to worship him, but he said, "You must not do that! I am a fellow-servant with you and your brothers who bear their witness to Jesus. It is God you must worship. For those who bear witness to Jesus have the spirit of prophecy"' (19.10), and 'When I had heard and seen them, I prostrated myself to worship the angel who had shown them [all these things] to me. But he said, "You must not do that! I am a fellow-servant with you and your brothers the prophets and with those who take to heart the words of this book. It is God you must worship"' (22.8–9). So long as we view the angels as fellow-workers, and in no way more important than we humans in the maintenance of our world, we will not go far wrong. Unfortunately, though, human nature desires glamour above all else, and so is attracted to phenomena rather than a voice that cries out in the wilderness, saying, 'Prepare the way for the Lord; clear a straight path for him' (Matthew 3.3). The angels are ambivalent creatures, at least in their separate forms, and can delude us instead of directing us to the divine source. It is certain that spirituality, our capacity to seek after God and to work his ways, should proceed *pari passu* with our investigation of the properties of angels, including our own guardian angel, who is a way of knowing the direction to God and our response to this, but no more divine than we ourselves are.

So should we concern ourselves with angels? We have already pointed out that such beings have been an increasing source of embarrassment to the modernistic type of theologian, who describes them as mythological. There is nothing especially derogatory about the concept of myth, which is simply a spiritual truth illustrated symbolically. Yet this definition implies that angels do not exist in an objective form, but are merely ideas in the mind of the percipient. In this view, they are a part of the great archetypal system of belief that constitutes much of the collective unconscious experience of humanity, so well delineated by Carl Gustav Jung. Such an archetypal experience may have a very therapeutic effect on the recipient, but it would be hard to substantiate the literal existence of an angelic being. This would be the view of an agnostic psychotherapist. Even to this day, there is controversy among Jungian therapists as to whether their master believed in the objective reality of God or whether he saw it as simply an intrapsychic formation that he called 'the self'. I personally believe that God is indeed immanent in the human soul in its highest and holiest part, which is traditionally called the spirit, or the 'apex of the soul'. This could indeed be similar to 'the self' that Jung describes. But I also hold that the transcendent God, who is beyond all rational knowledge and comes to us as pure love, makes contact with us through the spirit, where he is eternally present. The same scheme might apply to angels also. Yet many learned people have convinced themselves about the non-existence of angels, despite the growing number of books describing angelic encounters. My own view is that many of these reported encounters are quite genuine, and have had a distinctly beneficial effect on the person concerned.

The twentieth century is very much a century of apparitions – and UFO sightings are just one example. Jung believed that the flying saucer with its rounded contour was a classical mandala, and signified a soul seeking after wholeness. In other words, he believed that the UFO is an intrapsychic construct. Many people who claim to have seen UFOs would contest this viewpoint most strongly, and there are many investigators who accept the literal existence of UFOs. There are even people who believe that they have been abducted by the inhabitants of UFOs. Most psychotherapists will be incredulous concerning such claims, for they are well aware of the dramatizing capacity of the psyche – especially when it is unhappy; in this situation, anything that takes the individual away from the facts of the moment will be especially welcome. There is nothing dishonest in all this, only a *cri de cœur* of a somewhat disordered psyche; on the other hand, it may be that the phenomenon is of a demonic nature.

The problem of all parapsychology is to discern truth from fiction. One type of fiction is frank dishonesty, which implies a fabrication of the evidence, but a second type is a genuine misconstruing of what has been perceived. This fiction applies not only to the percipient, but also to the investigator. The integrity of parapsychology has been severely impugned by falsified research, although probably no more so than in other disciplines. However, whereas such claims in other disciplines are soon unmasked by parallel investigation, parapsychology is largely related to the analysis of reported phenomena that cannot be repeated quite so easily. In other words, parapsychology seeks to attain a scientific status; but until its phenomena are easily repeatable, there are many who will continue to dismiss its findings until they have personally had an encounter with the psychic dimension. Only a psychically sensitive investigator can penetrate this realm of human experience. Angels find their place here too. Incidentally, UFO expert Ivan Sanderson has suggested that why we have not been able to 'catch a UFO' is because they do not come from another planet, but from another set of dimensions. Thus when UFO forms travel into our space operating according to another set of laws, people see them differently, but the imaging power of the beholder always determines what is seen. This is quoted by G. Don Gilmore in a fascinating book called *Angels and Mortals: Their Co-creative Power*.[1] It could well be that the spaceman is the angel image most tractable to non-churchgoing members of the younger generation, a proposition hardly likely to be palatable to the traditional believer. In the end, though, what matters is the effect of an image on the spiritual evolution of the viewer: 'You will recognize them by their fruit' (Matthew 7.16). Some extraterrestrial communicators give a strong warning about the fate of humankind unless it radically changes its ways, and the truth of this cannot be faulted – even if it does smack of New Age teaching.

An apparition of another order entirely is that of the Virgin Mary, who has shown herself in a number of situations during the twentieth century. One famous apparition was at Fatima in Portugal in 1917, to three young, illiterate, shepherd children. The appearance was preceded by the manifestation of an angel, who seemed to be preparing the three for the appearance of Our Lady. She was described as 'A lady, dressed in a white garment that was brighter than the sun, emitting a light that was clearer and more intense than a cut-glass goblet full of crystal-clear water through which the strongest rays of the sun are shining ...' Yet it was the angel that gave the essential teaching, not the Madonna.

Another Marian apparition was seen by four children at Garabandal, near Santander in Spain, between 1961 and 1965. There were various phenomena. In the first instance, the Madonna appeared, bringing warning messages to the children and telling them what they should do; this was in 1961. A second message was relayed by the Archangel Michael in 1965: 'I, your mother, by the intercession of St Michael Archangel, bid you to mend your ways ... pray with sincerity, and whatever you ask will be granted ...'

A notable current apparition is that seen at Medjugorje in Bosnia, near the Croatian border. Six young visionaries have had direct communications with the Virgin Mary, and various psychical phenomena have caused a considerable sensation both among pilgrims and uncommitted visitors. Once again, angels have been mentioned. One of the visionaries, Ivanka, reported that Mary came to her with two angels. On another occasion, Jelena, a locutionary through whom the Virgin Mary spoke, saw and heard her guardian angel, and went on to describe other appearances of angels. In 1981, many people saw the sun spinning towards them for some fifteen minutes, disclosing angels with trumpets. This incident is known as the Miracle of the Sun.[2]

The messages received in these examples are very much what a proficient spiritual director would stress: constant prayer, attendance at the Eucharist, and a more disciplined life generally. Marian apparitions appeal most strongly to the Catholic temperament. A committed Protestant would be less likely to respond so enthusiastically, and the same would be true of those of other religious faiths. The angel assuredly comes from God, but we can clothe it in our own form. Catholic Christianity is more sympathetic to angels than is Protestantism, and so it is not surprising that nearly all the Marian appearances occur in Catholic areas. There have also been sightings in more neutral areas like Egypt, but here the focus was probably the Coptic Church, which was under persecution at that time (1968–71).

It should also be noted that the Virgin Mother is a notable archetype in the collective unconscious. In classical Greece and Rome, some of the heroes and legendary figures were believed to be conceived of a virginal mother, and also to undergo a physical resurrection after their death. The Christian would counter this damaging aspersion to their faith by seeing in the life and resurrection of Jesus a miraculous working out of archetypal material in the world of flesh and blood. In this way what appeared to be pure myth has now been realized in our world. One of Mary's other titles is 'Queen of Angels', and she herself is called the 'Angel of Peace'.

As we have already said, neither artists nor poets have been as reticent as theologians in accommodating angels. How wonderfully reassuring is the first verse of Richard Baxter's hymn:

Ye holy Angels bright,
Which stand before God's throne,
And dwell in glorious light,
Praise ye the Lord each one.
There you so nigh
Are much more meet
Than we the feet,
For things so high.

On a different level, but with a not dissimilar thought, comes
Francis Thompson's insight (from 'The Kingdom of God'):

The angels keep their ancient places;
Turn but a stone and start a wing!
'Tis ye, 'tis your estrangèd faces,
That miss the many-splendoured thing.[3]

A rather more wistful farewell to angels in the modern world
is contained in Robert Bridges's poem called 'Spirits':

Angel spirits of sleep,
White-robed, with silver hair,
In your meadows fair,
Where the willows weep,
And the sad moonbeam
On the gliding stream
Writes her scatter'd dream:

Angel spirits of sleep,
Dancing to the weir
In the hollow roar
Of its waters deep;
Know ye not how men say
That ye haunt no more
Isle and grassy shore
With your moonlit play;
That ye dance not here,
White-robed spirits of sleep,

All the summer night
Threading dances light?[4]

Yes indeed, the angels have been progressively banished from the company of sensible humans, but to what end? The answer would probably be 'truth', and this cannot be disregarded. No self-respecting person wants to cling on to an illusion, let alone rely on a type of idol. But let us hear what Rainer Maria Rilke has to say about angels in *The Duino Elegies*.

Who, if I cried out, might hear me — among the ranked
    Angels?
Even if One suddenly clasped me to his heart
I would die of the force of his being. For Beauty is only
the infant of scarcely endurable Terror, and we
are amazed when it casually spares us.
Every Angel is terrible.
And so I check myself, choke back my summoning
black cry. Who'll help us then? Not Angels,
Not Mankind; and the nosing beasts soon scent
how insecurely we're housed in this signposted World.

This is the beginning of the first elegy. The beginning of the second elegy has a somewhat similar ring:

Every angel is terror. I know it, yet still, alas!
I must sing you — you, great near-deadly birds
of the soul! Where have they gone, the days of Tobias
when one of those brilliant ones stood at the door
of the unexceptional house? Dressed for the journey
he was not at all terrible, a youth to a youth
who eagerly spied him. But should the Archangel —
dangerous, masked by the stars — should *he* tread
but a step lower and closer we should be struck down
by our hammering hearts. What *are* you?

Later in this second elegy Rilke asks:

Does then the cosmos in which we are gradually melting
not take a touch of our flavour? Not even
a taste of us? And the Angels, do they truly gather up
only their own ... what flows out from them?
Isn't some of our essence, sometimes, by chance,
gathered up with it?

Quoting David L. Miller, once more from *Angels and Mortals:
Their Co-creative Power*, Rilke was looking for a means of transforming visible things into invisibility, so that their essence might be retained at a deeper level of sensitivity. He wanted to transfigure visible earthly forms into their true essence, which might then be available to a more comprehensive psychical awareness. Rilke believed that this poetic act involved one with a 'terrible angel', a being who forced one to let go of things completely for this very purpose of transfiguration. The renunciation involved one in leaving things free from the grasp of the ego – such words as I, me, and mine – and praising them in words. And so he writes in the ninth elegy:

Were we put in this World here, truly, for speech? To say:
House, Fountain, Bridge, Gate, Jug, Fruit Tree; or Window?
Or even rise higher and say the word: Column?
Say: Tower? But to say these, remember,
to speak them ... in a manner that those things,
at heart, never intended to *be*? Could it be...
might not this be the World's cunning purpose,
speechlessly, secretly urging all lovers
so that each thing and all things themselves might
rejoice in the feelings they feel...?

Further on in the same elegy he writes:

And these things, whose own life is nourished by dying,
will hear how you praise and commend them, and, mortal,
entrust their survival to us, the most mortal of all;
willing us, wishing that we
in our hiddenest hearts might translate them

and take them – O World without end! – take them
into ourselves ... whatever our selves may finally be.[5]

The angel is the image of this experience. Rilke wrote to a
friend in 1923,

> The angel of the *Elegies* is that creature in which the trans-
> formation of the visible into invisibility, which we are
> accomplishing (in poetry), appears already fulfilled. For the
> angel of the *Elegies* all past towers and palaces are extant
> because long since invisible, and the still standing towers
> and bridges of our existence, *already* invisible, although (for
> us) they still physically continue. The angel of the *Elegies* is
> that being which stands security for recognizing in the
> invisible a higher degree of reality ... Therefore 'terrible' to
> us because we, its lovers and transformers, are still clinging
> to the visible ... All the worlds of the universe fling
> themselves into the invisible as into their next-deeper reality;
> *some stars heighten directly in intensity and pass away in the infinite
> consciousness of the angels ... others are dependent on creatures who
> slowly and laboriously transform them, in whose terror and ecstasy they
> reach their next invisible realization. We are*, be it emphasized once
> more, *in the sense of the Elegies we are these transformers of the earth:
> our whole existence, the flights and downfalls of our love, all capacitate
> us for the task* (beside which, essentially, no other holds).[6]

What all this means to me is that the angel brings spiritual
life, true spiritual body, into something that is as near lifeless
as one can dare to view anything. This applies horrifyingly to
the products of the pure reason, often called 'intellect' in our
modern terminology. Rational theology throughout the ages is
heavily tarred with this brush of unimaginative arrogance. It
does not move apart from the spirit of the age, useful as this
may be in seeing that it does not go ludicrously off course.
Yet how can the messenger figures that appear so consistently
in contemporary accounts of angelic visitations to disarmingly
ordinary people play this role of spiritual renewal? The angels
lighten the darkness of those whom they encounter, so that

these people begin to feel better physically, and to attain some degree of spiritual illumination. In other words, they bring something of God's presence into people's lives and also into the workings of the human mind. As such, I believe they are an essential part of the divine economy. They should work in complete harmony with the human intellect; an imbalance of either leads to a sentimental superstitiousness if the angels take charge and a heartless rationalism if the intellect runs human life.

A typical concept of an angel is that of a spiritual being gifted with intellect and free will, and superior to the human in its capacity to fulfil the divine purpose. This is a characteristically Aristotelian perspective, and was championed by Averroes (Ibn Rushd), the great Islamic philosopher (1126–98) of Spain and North Africa, who did so much to introduce Aristotelian philosophy to Jewish and Christian thinking. The crown of Christian Aristotelianism is St Thomas Aquinas (1225–74), whose *Summa Theologiae* and *Summa contra Gentiles* form the classical systematization of Roman Catholic theology. Thomas articulated the necessity for the existence of angels, inasmuch as they filled the gap between the rational human soul and God. Frederick Copleston, in his *History of Philosophy: Medieval Philosophy*, explains this more fully:

> We can discern the ascending orders or ranks of forms from the forms of inorganic substances, through vegetative forms, the irrational sensitive forms of animals, the rational soul of man, to the infinite and pure Act, God: but there is a gap in the hierarchy. The rational soul of man is created, finite and embodied, while God is uncreated, infinite and pure spirit; it is only reasonable, then, to suppose that between the human soul and God there are finite and created spiritual forms which are without body [i.e. Angels].[7]

Therefore, according to this point of view angels are without body and are logically necessary to a human knowledge of the embodiment of spirit.

Yet there is a contrasting view to the so-called necessity of angels. Here an earlier Islamic philosopher, Avicenna (Ibn Sina), who lived exclusively in Persia from 980 to 1037, is important. He too was a notable advocate of Aristotelian logic, in addition to being a physician of world repute; indeed, the scope of his knowledge and interests were those of a great genius. He split with Aristotelian logic on the very matter of the nature of angels. He disagreed with the traditional view that they were bodyless, and took the first steps upon a path of mystical theosophy that was to mark the direction that Islamic philosophy was to follow subsequently – especially in Persia and the other eastern lands of Islam. Whereas Averroes argued rationalistically and cosmologically, Avicenna, more than a century later, adopted a neo-Platonic and ontological (being concerned with the essence of things or being in the abstract) approach.

This neo-Platonic view is somewhat anticipated by the interpreting angel (*angelus interpres*) that we met in Chapter 2 in respect of the later Old Testament prophets Ezekiel, Zechariah, and Daniel, and that speaks interiorly and interprets the visions they see, and also in the angelic conversation that concludes the Book of Revelation (22.6–21). After telling John not to worship him, the angel says, 'I am coming soon, and bringing with me my recompense to repay everyone according to what he has done! I am the Alpha and the Omega, the first and the last, the beginning and the end' (verses 12–13). It is hard to distinguish between Jesus and his angel in this account. The neo-Platonic view is also anticipated in the early Christian tradition of the Trinity as angels.[8] It comes fully into its own in Plotinus, who hands it on to Proclus, who in turn inspired the pseudo-Dionysius (whose views on the angelic hierarchy we considered in Chapter 1), and from him, John Scotus Erigena. The last was an Irish theologian (*c.* 810–77), who was a fine mystic. He translated the writings of the pseudo-Dionysius and St Gregory of Nyssa, thus making them accessible to Western scholars. His writings were later condemned on a charge of pantheism – that is, the tendency to identify the creator with his creation.

The neo-Platonism of Plotinus entered Christian thought especially through St Augustine, whose writings influenced a number of medieval theologians. Among these were Alexander of Hales (1170/85–1245), who was born in Gloucestershire. He was basically an Augustinian, but had taken into account the psychological, physical, and metaphysical doctrines of Aristotle. In the matter of angels, however, he adopted a neo-Platonic stance, as did two more famous theologians of the school of Saint-Victor in Paris. The older was Hugh (1096–1141), an eminent scholastic theologian who began the tradition of mysticism that made the school of Saint-Victor famous throughout the twelfth century. The younger, and more important, was Richard, who was born in England or Scotland at an unknown date and died in 1173. He entered the Abbey of Saint-Victor and studied under Hugh, becoming prior in 1162. Though he wrote on the Trinity and the Scriptures, he is chiefly remembered for his works on mysticism. He is certainly one of the greatest Christian mystics, and had an influence that extended to the seventeenth century. Two later mystics who had a similar view about the nature of angels were Meister Eckhart (*c.* 1260–1327), who described angels as 'ideas of God', and Jakob Boehme (1575–1624), the greatest Protestant mystic.

It is evident that those of mystical temperament have had no difficulty in recognizing angels as manifestations of the divine presence, or at least the uncreated energies of God, given unreservedly to the whole cosmos. In this respect, it is of interest to consider Paul Tillich's views on angels, which side distinctly with the ontological and Platonic perspective:

> If you want to interpret the concept of Angels in a meaningful way today, interpret them as the Platonic essences, as the powers of being, not as special beings. If you interpret them in the latter way, it all becomes crude mythology. On the other hand, if you interpret them as emanations of the divine power of being in essences, in powers of being, the concept of Angels becomes meaningful and perhaps important ... The Angels are the spiritual mirror of the divine abyss – the essences in which the divine ground expresses itself.[9]

Elsewhere in his work, Tillich is even more concrete about angels. He writes, 'In our terminology we could say that the

Angels are concrete-poetic symbols of the structures or powers of being ... Their "epiphany" is a revelatory experience determining the history of religion and culture.'[10] He also writes, 'The rediscovery of angels from the psychological side as archetypes of the collective unconscious and the new interpretation of the demonic in theology and literature have contributed to the understanding of these powers of being, which are not beings (Aristotle's and Aquinas's 'separate intelligences'), but structures.'

All this is quoted from an article by David Miller,[11] in which he then makes the comment that angels are not *logically* necessary; they are *not* necessary as a category of creation in order that the rational mind may grasp the whole scheme. Yet they are necessary simply because they are what they *are* and not something else. G. Don Gilmore (see page 55) provides an excellent working definition of angels as those forms, images, or expressions through which the essences and energy forces of God can be transmitted. More succinctly, he says, an angel is a form through which a specific essence or energy can be transmitted for a specific purpose. The image or form of an angel is a creation of inspired imagination that is built up in group consciousness over the years by those who have visualized angels in a particular way. (Incidentally, Gilmore ministers at a Congregational church in the United States, while Miller holds a Chair of Professor of Religion – also in the United States.)

There is a tendency nowadays to 'psychologize' angels, to identify them exclusively with the archetypes of the collective unconscious. While this may be an accurate enough assessment on a particular occasion, we should always be wary of the tendency towards reductionism, ascribing a spiritual phenomenon to nothing but some quirk of the mind, that is so much a feature of our time. That which can be reduced to the measure of our understanding can be conveniently manipulated, but in the process its own integrity and life are destroyed, and it becomes merely a plaything of the psyche. Paul Tillich himself may have over-identified angels with psychological archetypes. It is much more probable that an angel reveals itself through the archetypal apparatus of the unconscious; in addition, though, there may be an incontrovertible physical presence that testifies to its objective reality in our very material world of phenomena.

In the next two chapters, we will examine the interaction of angel and human in the demonic dimension.

6
Angels of Darkness

❖❖❖

An especially challenging feature of the angelic group is its moral ambivalence. The angels of light who are the messengers of God's will are well delineated, but what about the powers of darkness that may lead us to hatred, chaos, and ultimate destruction? These are the demonic spirits that also work in the vast cosmic realm. In biblical times, the existence and power of these elements was largely taken for granted. In the Gospels, Jesus is frequently portrayed in the role of casting out devils, so that people with physical and mental ailments might be healed. It must be frankly admitted, however, that the precise nature of the individual's complaint often eludes diagnosis. Yet Jesus himself had no doubt that in some instances the person's illness was directly related to a demonic attack — so much so that he commissioned his disciples to heal the sick, raise the dead, cleanse lepers, and drive out demons (Matthew 10.8). We now believe that the leprosy of biblical times was a congeries of different skin diseases, while 'the dead' were much more often in a state of spiritual darkness than at the end of their bodily life — there were only three resurrection miracles attributed to Jesus himself, those of Jairus' daughter, the widow of Nain's son, and Lazarus, a small collection when compared with his healing work among the living.

Nowadays, demonic spirits — no less than their shining angelic counterparts — have fallen under severe prohibition, and not without good reason. We now acknowledge that physical disease follows a basic disturbance of function consequent on such clear-cut factors as infection, malnutrition, impaired blood supply, nervous dysfunction or malignancy, to name only a few common causes. Once these conditions are properly treated (a situation becoming increasingly more possible year by year as medical knowledge advances), there may be a return to a previous state of health.

In the record of Jesus' healing practice, there are only three references to demonic affliction causing a frankly bodily disorder: the dumb man of Matthew 9.32–3, the dumb and blind man of Matthew 12.22, and the epileptic boy of Mark 9.14–29, with parallel accounts in Matthew and Luke. While one should avoid being dogmatic, I personally suspect that any demonic influence in the first two cases was merely a coincidental factor affecting a person who already had a physical disorder. Epilepsy is known to be a result of a periodic disturbance of function of part of the brain, and can usually be controlled with anticonvulsant drugs. These may put an end to the fits without necessarily abolishing the fundamental disturbance; indeed, a patient is often advised to continue taking medication indefinitely lest the fits recur. I have little difficulty in accepting that a demonic attack may precipitate a fit in a predisposed person, but if Jesus did in fact effect a complete cure, he did something more that merely deliver a demonic spirit to God's care.

The bulk of Jesus' copious healing miracles were the result of an enormous energy, or power, that seemed to pour out from his person. This is in fact the Holy Spirit, which is the medium of all healing, and works in those with a special gift – irrespective of their belief system. However, whereas a person who is purely psychically based is very liable to fall victim to an egotistical or gnostic domination (believing that occult knowledge can lead to salvation from the world's ills), the truly spiritual person, one who offers their gift to God as a sacrifice for the sake of all creation, will rise ever more gloriously in the knowledge of the Most High and his angels. When one studies Jesus' remarkable healing power, one can hardly fail to see that he was the source of an enormous emission of the Holy Spirit; and I believe that the angels of light are closely involved in such profoundly transforming remedial work.

If the demonic spirits have a typical manifestation, and this is especially obvious to psychically sensitive people, it lies in the production of an unaccountably unpleasant atmosphere. This may infest a particular locality, or be present around an unfortunate victim. Yet all this can easily be put down to coincidence, or even a simple misreading of the situation. Did not Job himself remind his wife, right at the beginning of his own agony, that if we accept the good things of God, we must also be prepared to face evil from him also (Job 2.9–10)! Admittedly, the patience of that noble man began to run out as the pain increased in magnitude and showed no signs of remitting; but in the end he grasped something about the wonder of the creation and organization of the world that he had previously taken for granted. Its wonder had almost entirely escaped him – a situation that we too confront when our pleasant little world is harshly cut away from under our feet by misfortune, and we are obliged to inspect our existence with the realism of an aware adult. In the Job story, misfortune was indeed produced by Satan, the adversary, but under the aegis of God, the creator of Job and Satan alike. In fact, Satan, or the devil (the accuser in the context of law-court procedure), does not figure very often in the Old Testament canon, and although he is a figure of malice and hatred, he still works as one of God's servants, as part of the heavenly court – so well portrayed in Job 1.6–12 and 2.1–7.

In addition, Satan occurs in three other places in the Old Testament: Psalm 109.6 ('Put up some rogue to denounce him, an accuser to confront him'), I Chronicles 21.1 ('Now Satan, setting himself up against Israel, incited David to make a census of the people'), and Zechariah 3.1–2 ('Then he showed me Joshua the high priest standing before the angel of the Lord, with Satan standing at his right hand to accuse him. The angel said to Satan, "The Lord silence you, Satan! May the Lord, who has chosen Jerusalem, silence you! Is not this man a brand snatched from the fire?"'). It is interesting that the corresponding passage to the one in I Chronicles – namely 2 Samuel 24.1 – blames God directly for inciting David to make the census. At that stage of Israelite history, all phenomena were attributed to God, since 'secondary causes' were not recognized. The Books of Samuel and Kings reached their final form just before the time of the Babylonian exile, at the beginning of the sixth century before Christ, whereas the Books of Chronicles were probably written, with Ezra and Nehemiah, during the third century before Christ. By this time, Satan the Accuser was clearly a much more malicious figure.

Another passage of interest in our investigation into the origin and properties of the dark angels is found in Isaiah 14.12–17:

> Bright morning star, how you have fallen from heaven, thrown to earth, prostrate among the nations! You thought to yourself: 'I shall scale the heavens to set my throne high above the mighty stars; I shall take my seat on the mountain where the gods assemble in the far recesses of the north. I shall ascend beyond the towering clouds and make myself like the Most High!' Instead you are brought down to Sheol, into the depths of the abyss. Those who see you stare at you, reflecting as they gaze: 'Is this the man who shook the earth, who made kingdoms quake, who turned the world into a desert and laid its cities in ruins, who never set his prisoners free?'

The morning star, also called Lucifer, was identified by the Fathers of the Church as the prince of the demons. In this passage he was symbolized and represented by a pagan tyrant, probably as Assyrians such as Sargon II or Sennacherib, and supplemented in the period of the exile by a king of Babylon, who would have been Nebuchadnezzar or Nabonidus. This passage is the farthest we may stretch for a biblical allusion to the myth of the fall of the angels under the self-centred arrogance of a very powerful archangel whom we call Lucifer – possibly Satan and the devil are aspects of this perverse creature. A rather similar passage, but less explicit, is spoken against the King of Tyre in Ezekiel 28.11–19. In each of these instances, the fall of a vicious tyrant is compared with the fall of the angels, but here the comparison ends: the tyrants disappear except in the annals of history, while the fallen angels remain extremely powerful in producing havoc.

Demons, which are usually synonymous with the devil, or devils, assume the form of a serpent in the story of the Fall in Genesis 3. This is also the case in Isaiah 27.1: 'On that day the Lord with his cruel sword, his mighty and powerful sword, will punish Leviathan, that twisting sea serpent, that writhing serpent Leviathan; he will slay the monster of the deep.' The Book of Leviticus contains interesting references to demons; in Leviticus 7.17 we read that the people are no longer to offer their slaughtered beasts to the demons whom they wantonly follow, a commandment blatantly disregarded by the renegade King of Israel, Jeroboam, who appointed 'his own priests for the shrines, for the demons, and for the calves which he had made' (2 Chronicles 11.15). These last two were of course merely idols. Of decidedly greater interest is a reference to Azazel in Leviticus 16.8–10 with regard to a primitive atonement ritual. The priest had to cast lots over two chosen he-goats, one to be for God and the other for Azazel; the goat on which the lot for the Lord had fallen was to be dealt with as a purification-offering, but the goat on which the lot for Azazel had fallen was to be made to stand alive before the Lord, for expiation to be made over it, before it was driven away into the wilderness to Azazel – who appears, according to ancient Hebrew and Canaanite belief, to have been a demon who lived in the desert. This is the barren region where God does not exert his life-giving activity. The goat is dedicated to Azazel, not sacrificed to him, and it then bears away the sins of the people to his desert haunts.

The demonic element is clearly not a common feature of the Old Testament, and often gives the impression of being a theological artifice rather than a living being. By contrast, the demons plays a considerable part in the New Testament. They appear thirty-five times in the New Testament, of which fifteen are Gospel entries. They are much less theological hypotheses, and much more active entities. The probable reason for this different approach and emphasis is a general growth of under-standing, and the extreme psychic sensitivity of Jesus and his brilliance as an exorcist. In other words, the demonic spirits were as prevalent in the time of the Old Testament as sub-sequently, but the general run of the people and their ministers were oblivious of their baneful influence on the history of the people before the great exile to Babylon. Perhaps even the notable prophets were impervious to demonic activity. My own experience in the field has shown me that while many people may be demonically assailed, they have only a very blurred idea that all is not well. Fully aware ministers of deliverance are rare individuals; their value cannot be over-emphasized, but their sufferings can be quite terrible, for their sensitivity puts them in the front-line of demonic assault – especially when they are actively involved in their specialized work. The general incredulity of their peers does not lessen their burden – though when things in life go seriously wrong, an increasing number of people gravitate to such ministers for assistance.

As I have already indicated, the demonic spirit shows itself by its capacity to assail the mental and emotional equilibrium of its victim. This it does in two ways: first, by affecting the psyche directly – perhaps by producing a state bordering on clinical depression in a previously stable person, or by accentuating and complicating the symptoms of one who is already mentally ill; and secondly, by precipitating a never-ending sequence of misfortunes. Such misfortunes tend to aggravate the emotional affliction, which in turn exposes the individual to more misfortune. In the great majority of instances, the spirit does not actually possess, or take over, the personality of its victim, but it either infests it at close contact, or else attacks it from a distance (as far as one can use the language of space in a relationship that is psychic, and therefore beyond time and space as we understand these terms on an earthly level). The more intense the infestation, the more severe are the mental and emotional effects, whereas demonic attacks somewhat removed from the person lead to variable mental and emotional distress and the tendency for things to go wrong on an unprecedented scale. I have yet to encounter a frankly possessed person, but what is described by those who have had this experience is a complete intolerance to Christian conversation or the presence of Christian religious symbols, and a tendency to fall into a trance-like state when blessed or prayed for. In this state, the voice may be abnormal and the language may be one unknown to the person in their normal state (this is called xenoglossia). When confronted by the minister, there may be a show of supernatural strength, and there may also be extraordinary powers of clairvoyance – such that the person is able to recount accurately events happening at a distance in time or space completely unknown to them.[1]

In the more usual work with infested or attacked people, the physical response to ministry is usually minimal, but occasionally there may be a dramatic outburst or a falling to the ground with a rapid restoration of equilibrium. However, the lack of a severe physical reaction may be psychically transferred to the minister, who is attacked not so much at the time of deliverance (except in particularly vicious cases), but later on. Bedtime is a period of great vulnerability to demonic activity; when the minister of deliverance is asleep, the unconscious lies enticingly open to invasions of all kinds. Freud called dreams the 'royal road to the unconscious', but this process can also be assailed by extraneous material that Freud may not have been prepared to acknowledge as psychic invasion from a demonic source. The more open-minded Jung would probably have been more sympathetic to this possibility. When one is demonically attacked in this way, one awakens as from a nightmare that exposes a dread with which the conscious mind would normally be able to cope quite easily. At this point, one's world shakes under a stark feeling of the futility of all things and the awful awareness of extinction of everything when one dies; normally there would at least be a little hope, but now all is enveloped in darkness. In a completely unprotected person, the state could progress rapidly to panic attacks or even a mounting depression.

The minister of deliverance must know how to cut short this assault at once by commanding the demonic spirit to leave the individual and the whole earthbound plane. The spirit is not simply allowed to drift around aimlessly, but is sent directly to God's care for protection and healing. When one is awakened in the early hours of the morning in this state of terror, a personal deliverance effects a speedy relief, and then one can eventually return to sleep. Yet the attack may occur later on; if one is about to awaken for the day's work, it is still necessary to perform a personal deliverance, and then rest even for a brief spell; if not, a most unpleasant aura of unease may permeate one's daily work, which could do quite a measure of harm.

In all that I have written, I speak from strictly personal experience. It is a rule that if one is attempting to do good work, one is sure to be especially assailed by demonic forces. It is essential for the minister of deliverance to be supported by the prayers of many concerned people; and if he or she can work in close collaboration with someone else, so much the better. Such a person should, in my experience, have a strong Christian faith and be acutely sensitive psychically. A combination like this is not as common as it ought to be, largely because of the prejudice many Christians still harbour against anything that goes by the name 'psychic'.

How, though, does one know that there is a demonic spirit causing trouble? The answer is that one senses it by the reaction it produces in one emotionally. Discernment of spirits is among St Paul's list of gifts of the Spirit (1 Corinthians 12.10), though the context here is the ability to distinguish true spirits from false, rather than knowing that a demonic spirit is present in a locality. Discernment is seen in the context of Old Testament prophecy – for instance, Elijah and the prophets of Baal (1 Kings 18.21–40); Micaiah discerning the lying spirit in the mouths of the prophets counselling the wicked King Ahab to fight against the Aramaeans (1 Kings 22.13–28); and especially the dramatic encounter between Jeremiah and Hananiah, the false prophet, that occupies the twenty-eighth chapter of the Book of Jeremiah. If one has this gift of discernment, one simply knows that things are not what they appear; on the whole, women are more acute psychically than are men, and this applies to the discernment of demonic spirits also. I was fortunate enough to work in close collaboration with such a gifted woman until her death at a very advanced age; I now have to do the work on my own, but I strongly believe her spirit helps me both in discernment and in dangerous deliverance situations. In the end, it is God alone who is one's guardian and help, so that a dedicated prayer life is mandatory both for one's own protection and for the success of the work. I have no doubt that a clear conscience is a great asset in the deliverance ministry, for then one's mind is not distracted by any feeling of inadequacy. No one, however, is morally perfect; furthermore we are all subject to prejudice against certain types of people, no matter how vigorously we may deny this on a conscious level.

For this reason, some impersonal means of confirming one's suspicions of demonic attack is in my opinion essential. I personally use the tossing of a previously blessed coin as my means of confirming both my inner spiritual diagnosis, and for ascertaining whether my deliverance ministry has been successfully completed. The head of the coin I take as positive and the tail as negative. I need hardly add that one should do this work of discernment only in a condition of rapt prayer; the Lord's Prayer is always the focus of my attention, since I cannot imagine any more perfect prayer than this. But one must be able to address God as directly as one would one's most intimate friend, and the mind should not wander. All this takes years of assiduous practice, simple as it may sound in print. Some readers may argue that the use of a physical object smacks of divination; yet it must be remembered that the use of lots is mentioned throughout the Bible – a good New Testament example is the choice of Matthias to replace Judas Iscariot, so that he might be elected an apostle with the other eleven (Acts 1.23–6). It is not the means that are important, but the motivation behind their use. If they are used selfishly, they will reap a harvest of destruction; but if used altruistically, there is no reason why they too cannot be incorporated into the divine purpose. God is, after all, the master of all creation.

In any such test as I have described, there is always the danger of interference, such that a false answer is given. If what is shown goes counter to one's deeper intuition, one must challenge in the name of Jesus Christ. Sometimes a number of tests have to be made before one is relatively sure of the truth of the answer provided. As in all work on a psychic level, mischievous incursion is inevitably a problem; but if there is a truly spiritual oversight, the correct directive will be provided. In my own experience, I have been gratified how often the answer has been clearly right in terms of the healing produced by the deliverance work. Yet as in all other activities in our mysterious universe, there is no one final infallible answer, and errors are part of our way of growth into deeper knowledge and truth. If anything can be relied on, it is the spirit of love, for this is closest to God, whom we may only know through his uncreated, outflowing energies, of which the angels are an important part if we accept the more mystical view of their genesis.

Secondly, what predisposes an individual to demonic attack? This again can be answered only on a relatively superficial external level. Those who meddle thoughtlessly with psychic things, such as an impious incursion into the occult dimension, are obvious candidates for attack. The interdictions against sorcery and necromancy found in the Bible (Leviticus 19.31 and Deuteronomy 18.10–11 are standard texts) are a sensible precaution against this danger; in addition, they prevent an intermediate entity usurping the function and very person of God in the eyes of an ignorant person. In a rather similar way, the same kind of misgiving applies to the practitioners of magic, which may be defined as the invocation of angelic or demonic spirits for essentially self-determined ends: 'black' magic, which invokes the demonic group, is clearly evil, but even 'white' magic, which invokes angels or personal spirits, is not without its adverse side. Though many white magicians are well intentioned (believing that they are working for the good of nature as well as their fellow humans, and not in an attitude of ruthless domination), their individualistic interference in the workings of nature brings them into contact with demonic spirits as part of the price they pay for their arrogance. By contrast, the world's higher religions are more closely linked to God, however he may be conceived (remembering that whatever one says about God is untrue, as Meister Eckhart exclaimed), and so there is at least some humility and a tendency to pray contemplatively rather than to command; to listen rather that to assert oneself. In all this, we can see the great difference between the psychic dimension and the spiritual one.

People with some types of mental illness are also in my experience liable to demonic attack. Sufferers of schizophrenia appear to be especially prone to attack, but sometimes it is an intractable depression that makes one vulnerable. Not infrequently, an efficient deliverance ministry has a rapidly impressive effect in ameliorating suffering without curing the fundamental disorder of the brain, probably a chemical disturbance. Therefore the fundamental condition is not a result of demonic attack, but rather some dysfunction of the brain. This must be stressed, because some enthusiastic exorcists believe that their ministrations can totally cure mental illness, so that further medical treatment is unnecessary. When there is a recurrence of the illness, the patient may then feel guilty that they have 'let in' another demonic spirit — even to the extent of delaying a consultation with their doctor until they are seriously ill. It is evident that a close collaboration between psychiatrists on the one hand and ministers of deliverance on the other would be distinctly helpful to a number of mentally ill people; but there would have to be humility and a willingness to learn on the part of both practitioners. Those people who believe that they are spiritually 'advanced' can be just as intolerant as some members of the scientific fraternity!

The manifestation of demonic spirits can vary from a severe mental and emotional attack to something that is quite subtle and subjective; people around the afflicted individual are aware that all is not well, but cannot understand what is wrong. Unlike a mentally deranged person, both the personality and the cognitive (knowing) and affective (feeling) functions of the mind are intact. There is no delusion of persecution, such as is found in paranoid individuals (a part of the schizophrenic illness in some cases). The demonically attacked person simply cannot bear the atmosphere both within and around them, with many being quite articulate about the cause of the trouble. If they are dismissed as mentally ill, they can indeed proceed to a depressive state that will not remit until a deliverance ministry is performed.

Unquiet spirits of the dead, also called earthbound spirits, may produce physical phenomena in the environment that can terrify the person who experiences them. Quite often these phenomena, such as audible footsteps, interference with the electricity supply, and mischievous turning on of taps to name but a few, are essentially SOS signals by the unquiet spirit who is seeking release into the greater world of God's love, but is held back by feelings of guilt or fear. A typical instance of this came to my attention some twenty years ago when I started work in my present parish. A young woman was experiencing physical phenomena in her newly purchased flat, and she called on my help as her parish priest. Both of us were acutely psychic, and it became clear that the spirit was that of a notorious murderer who had been executed some thirty years earlier and who had worked in the neighbourhood. He could not accept God's unconditional forgiveness, after having paid the supreme penalty for his crime, and was immobilized by guilt. I gave him absolution at once, something I do routinely to unquiet spirits if I am shown that they require it, and the spirit was immediately released. At once, the flat became quiet and orderly.

I mention the effects of the unquiet 'dead' simply to contrast their presence with those of demonic spirits. The effects of unquiet spirits are sometimes not unlike the common poltergeist that arises from misdirected sexual energy, usually emanating from adolescent boys and girls, which is converted into psychic energy. Sometimes unquiet spirits can also produce an atmosphere of unhappiness both in the local environment and in the person directly involved, but there is little of the more profound mental and emotional distress so often found with demonic infestation or attack.

Another factor to be noted here is that demonic spirits do not seem to possess the idioplastic qualities of the bright angels. They do not appear in a visible form such as the winged figures or the indistinguishable human agents often encountered as angelic apparitions. However, as we noted in the last chapter, it is conceivable that the encounters with spacefolk who supposedly abduct their victims (and even cohabit with them to give birth to children – who have not as yet been produced for general scrutiny!), may be an aspect of demonic materialization. In Chapter 3, the Letter of Jude was mentioned in respect of angels who were not content to maintain the dominion assigned to them, but abandoned their proper dwelling-place (verse 6). According to Genesis 6.1–4, the angels lusted after women of the earth, and children were born to them. It was this sin that precipitated the story of Noah and the Flood. Is this contemporary belief a realization of an ancient myth, or is it pure psychopathology in emotionally disturbed people with a strong imagination and a degree of psychic

7

The Light
and the Darkness

❖❖❖

'God is light, and in him there is no darkness at all.' We began our thoughts with this celebrated statement from I John 1.5, but now we have to qualify this with what we know about the demonic dimension in the angelic hierarchy – to say nothing of that in human nature. The Genesis allegory insists that everything God made was good; this applies to the human creation no less than the animal creation: 'God created human beings in his own image; in the image of God he created them; male and female he created them' (Genesis 1.27). One may, I feel, include the angelic hierarchy in this general category of excellence. If we take the Aristotelian view of their nature, as in some way bridging the gap between the human and God himself, there is no reason why they should not have started their career as impeccable creatures. If we can accept the more mystical view that they are forms, images, or expressions through which the essences and energy forces of God can be transmitted, a definition we encountered in Chapter 5, then it seems beyond belief that these could assume a demonic character such as I have described in the last chapter.

Let us say at once that no human being can give an authoritative answer to this enigma. The weakness of the Aristotelian approach is its very accessibility: it is only too easy to make the angels anthropomorphic images who are subject to the same temptations as we humans in our life on earth. One explanation is a fall of the angels under the hubris of a particularly impressive angel called Lucifer, who has succeeded in attracting a number of his fellows under his banner. We considered the scriptural evidence, or rather the lack of it, in the last chapter. The other explanation that we have also thought about is the lust of some angels for especially beautiful women, as described in Genesis 6.1–4. Not surprisingly, God was outraged by this perversion, and vowed to destroy the whole human race apart from Noah and his family. If angels are in truth rather similar in psychology to humans, these myths are not to be disregarded, for they seem to arise from the collective unconscious that envelops and informs all of us of deep cosmic truths that normally could not penetrate the busy conscious mind intent on getting as much for the individual as possible.

However, I suspect that we are meant to broaden our conception of what actually is good for us, and what God may be challenging us to undertake and to become. If, for instance, we consider the allegory of the Fall seriously, but not fundamentalistically, it becomes increasingly evident that God sent the serpent, the devil, to tempt Adam and Eve. It is even more evident that the outcome was not only expected by God, but actually orchestrated by him. What child, if commanded absolutely by its parent to avoid something, to refrain from a special course of action, to ignore a very real focus of craving planted in its very midst, could possibly resist the temptation? If God had simply ignored the whole issue, it is very probable that Adam and Eve would have remained oblivious of the special tree with its fruit of the knowledge of good and evil. They would have lived on in happy ignorance in the country of paradise, perhaps even to this day, though of course there is no knowledge of time or space in that delectable realm. In other words, Adam and Eve would have remained in childlike ignorance, completely unaware of the beauty and magnificence of the terrain they were privileged to inhabit. 'Where ignorance is bliss, 'tis folly to be wise', wrote Thomas Gray in the 'Ode on a Distant Prospect of Eton College'.

Yet humans are not born to remain in the bliss of ignorance. Everything in the pattern of human growth and development militates against this comfortable complacency that produces a stifling inertia and leads to nowhere in particular. It could, of course, be argued that if Adam and Eve had had the inner discipline and patience to abide by the divine interdiction and eschew the forbidden fruit, they might have grown up sufficiently in due course for the ban to be lifted. Then they would have been able to understand the nature of good and evil in truly divine terms, and their will would have coincided with that of God. Certainly it is true that when humans take the law into their own hands, the results are frequently demonic in nature and intensity. But how will we ever know what is the divine way to perfect behaviour and relationships with the other creatures in our environment, to say nothing of the greater world in which we try to make our contribution? It seems that experience is the key to wisdom.

The real issue is between the will and the imagination. E. Coué made the paradoxical statement that when the will and the imagination come into conflict, the imagination wins. As Roberto Assagioli writes in his book *Psychosynthesis*,[1] Coué's statement is an empirical and paradoxical way of expressing an important law of psychological life: 'Every image has in itself a motor-drive' or 'Images and mental pictures tend to produce the physical conditions and the external acts corresponding to them'. The power of images is well recognized by propagandists, while advertisers are keenly aware of the motor-power of imagination – or what they more vaguely call 'suggestion' – and utilize it abundantly, and often very ably.

The human is gifted with a strong will that is potentially free. This freedom, which is a high peak of human achievement, comes only with long experience that embraces both the civilization of the race and the education of the individual. Thus early on in life, our activities are liable to misdirection by the power of those around us; our parents and teachers should be able to direct us in the right direction, but often they fail because of their own inadequacy. However, as we come to adult stature, we have to follow our own way. If the centre of spiritual identity within the psyche, called the soul or true self, is in command, we will indeed work from a focus of free will. But many people are still liable to seduction by images implanted into their minds from external sources because they are purely ego-centred. In such a state, what they will desire most is pure personal gratification. This was the precise situation of Adam and Eve. God had forbidden them to perform a certain deed, yet not provided them with the means of repelling the subversive imagination implanted in their minds by the angel of darkness. When they were tempted, their fall was inevitable. This is the universal human condition.

To me, it seems much more probable that God organized the serpent to give Adam and Eve the necessary shove towards self-actualization; their awareness of their nakedness after eating the forbidden fruit, so that they fashioned loincloths made from fig leaves to conceal their sexual organs, is a manifestation of their separate self-awareness. This is not necessarily to be sought in itself, but it is an inevitable step in the right direction of personal responsibility which should end in a collective caring for all that lives. When poor Adam and Eve are expelled from the Garden of Eden, a lovely metaphor for the paradisical state, they are commencing their long journey back, but this time as adult members of the world order; a situation that we still envisage after countless generations of hope followed by despair, of disillusion fertilized by new hope that leads to an altered way of life. Certainly the biblical narrative on the one hand, and the twentieth century on the other, illustrate these trends with startling accuracy and pitiful aspiration. Will we never move beyond the darkness to the full appreciation of the light?

In his 'Ode on Intimations of Immortality', William Wordsworth speaks of the 'Soul that rises with us, our life's Star', having 'elsewhere its setting', and coming from afar: not in entire forgetfulness, and not in utter nakedness, but trailing clouds of glory do we come from God, who is our home. He recounts with almost unbearable poignancy the gradual successive withdrawal of the heavenly vision from the infant, the boy, even the youth, until the man 'perceives it die away', and fade into the light of day. This is no sentimental outpouring from a great poet of the Romantic period of the late eighteenth and early nineteenth centuries. It is a true assessment of the inner world of not a few articulate young children. Those destined to succumb shortly to malignant disease of various types seem to be especially mature spiritually, to the extent of caring more about their grief-stricken parents than their own suffering.

Yet even young children who are not ill can sometimes startle one with their spiritual perspicacity. Why, it may be asked, do such spiritually aware children have to grow up like the boy in Wordsworth's poem? Why does their spiritual vision have to become blurred and distorted as they enter a world of darkness, of crass materialism where self-satisfaction is advertised as the *summum bonum* of all true success, where salacious entertainment is blared out in the very streets? It is easy enough to blame the fallen nature of the human for these moral and spiritual atrocities. Even religion seems to have brought quite as much cruelty and destruction into the world as love and enlightenment. The reason for this apparent paradox lies in the universal human desire for absolute assurance; so long as a religious institution can appear to provide this assurance, its members may be fully prepared to bow down to the power structure inherent in that establishment. And so the human mind allows itself to be enslaved by a more powerful organization, while it basks in an assurance that may well be illusory. Only those who have the courage to search for themselves according to the capacity of the mind and soul that God has given them are likely to come to a truth that really does set them free from human illusion, a truth inseparable from the way Jesus showed in his life among us.

Who ultimately is responsible for the sorry state of affairs on earth, remembering that it seems to have been part of life right from the beginning of creation (if one takes the allegory of Noah and the Flood seriously)? The first culprit is obviously the human being. In the early chapters of Genesis, the sins of humanity serve to pervert nature until a state of enmity prevails among the animals and between them and the human. In the glorious vision of Isaiah 11.6–9, the advent of a distant paradisical peace between all creatures is described, and St Paul makes this a practical proposition following the incarnation and resurrection of Christ:

> For I reckon that the sufferings that we now endure bear no comparison with the glory, as yet unrevealed, which is in store for us. The created universe is waiting with eager expectation for God's sons to be revealed. It was made subject to frustration, not of its own choice but by the will of him who subjected it, yet with the hope that the universe

itself is to be freed from the shackles of mortality and is to enter upon the glorious liberty of the children of God (Romans 8.18–21).

In the fallen state of the human – that is, the person who follows the disobedience to the divine command – the dark angels find a hospitable place of residence. God gave human beings the will to choose, which is the basis of free will, long before they were able to discern good from evil, and so it would seem, at least in viewing the matter superficially, that the human race brought the sorry state upon itself and, by extension, on the world too.

But where was God when all this was happening? Were not his creatures well-made, according to the Genesis story? It becomes increasingly probable that God himself cannot be exonerated from the chaos that followed, that indeed he had a major part in the proceedings, unless he was either a faulty creator or else one whose concern in his creation soon lapsed, rather like a vendor who left his article with the purchaser and then went away indefinitely. The Jews have had the fundamental insight that their God is always alive, the living God in fact. This was what Jesus meant when he reminded the Sadducees, who maintained that there was no resurrection because the doctrine was not to be found in the teaching of Moses, that God had indeed revealed the doctrine to him when Moses met him in the apparition of the burning bush: 'I am the God of Abraham, the God of Isaac, the God of Jacob', for 'He is not God of the dead but of the living' (Mark 12.26–7).

God is indeed eternally alive, and is closer to his creation than its own self-awareness. Yet at the same time an enormous distance separates the two; the divine transcendence allows the creature to get on with its own affairs without God interfering like an over-solicitous parent of the old school, never letting its children live their own lives. If God's creation were anything other than perfect, he would be available like an artisan to put the mechanism right, but instead he has arranged a self-perpetuating universe that may hold out for many million years, by which time we may hope that the second coming of Christ may have altered the very scheme of reality.

And yet can we really call the earth a perfect abode for humans? Apart from natural disasters like earthquakes, volcanoes, floods, hurricanes, and droughts, there are the various diseases that afflict all forms of life. Many infections have come under increasing control (though AIDS remains a notable exception), but the degenerative diseases of later life, and also cancer, continue to take their toll. On the other hand, who would really want to reach an advanced age if the quality of living was seriously vitiated by dementia, blindness, deafness, or paralysis? The wise person realizes that it is these very impediments that set the seal on human greatness, for when we are diminished beyond previous recognition, something of the fully diminished man on the cross shows himself in us. What indeed is God saying to us? If we take Christ as our paradigm, we may begin to see what our pattern of life ought to be; and how in our striving for that perfection that follows human understanding we may evade the encounter with a God who is as much master of evil as of goodness, of pain as of pleasure, of darkness as of light.

It cannot be denied that God is the ultimate cause of evil, by which I mean the power that seeks to destroy all creation and produce total chaos (using the word in its theological context as a formless void out of which God effected the creation, described in Genesis I.2). It starts by destroying human happiness and ends as an agent of death — personal, communal, and finally universal. The advent and effects of fascism in this century speak more eloquently of its results than anything that could be put down in words. And yet God, 'the maker of all that is, seen and unseen' (to quote the beginning of the Nicene Creed), is necessarily the effector of evil also; certainly it would not have come about had he been more careful in the creation of his cosmos! If he had not given his prize creature, the human being, a high degree of intelligence, combined with a great power of imagination and a free will, there would have been a sheep-like subservience to the divine will, the forbidden fruit would have remained uneaten, and we would all be mouldering in paradise. If only we had been given a really safe world in which to live and without diseases to trouble us, we could have gone on living to the age spans described in respect of the earliest patriarchs in the first chapters of the Book of Genesis!

However, our whole lifespan would have been spent in sleep, for where there is no challenge there is no movement, let alone growth. If only God had planted that wretched tree bearing the fruit of the knowledge of good and evil elsewhere, he need not have spent any time warning us not to tamper with it! And if he insisted on planting the tree, he could at least have excluded from its ambience that nasty serpent, the very symbol of all that is evil in his creation, and what we now call the devil. And who created that serpent if not God? Indeed, he is described as one of the members of the court of heaven in Job 1.6, and plays a vital role in Job's spiritual education. Without the devil's role as legal adversary, Job would have remained a kind-hearted, pious man who loved an image of God, while being quite distant from the God of Abraham, Isaac, and Jacob whom Jesus spoke about, and who Blaise Pascal experienced in his celebrated mystical vision.

This rather lighthearted diversion brings us to the heart of the matter. The presence of what we call evil in the world is no fortuitous circumstance, nor can it be summarily laid at the feet of self-willed humans who would then simply be prime-movers in the strange sequence. Evil is an integral part of creation, as much a reality as what we call good, and we have to learn to live creatively with the whole. The *via media* between the extremes of a stultifying goodness and a destroying evil is a balance that can use all circumstances in life constructively. Needless to say, all this is far more easily said than done. Our present century, now drawing gratefully to a breathless close, has taught us a great deal about this way forward.

There are two very well-known parables of Christ that can help us on our journey. First there is the sad decline of the prodigal son (Luke 15.11–32). He quitted his patrimony in a state of elation allied to fierce independence, taking all the money to a distant country where he spent it profligately. In the end, though, the once-presentable young man was reduced to a pitiable state of dereliction. He had squandered his particular talents, and now all that was left was his own wretched presence. In that presence he saw who he really was, both a fool and the son of a rich father. His independence had been eroded by his stupidity, his pride by his distress, and so he could return in abject failure to his father whose presence he had once dismissed so lightly. He said, 'I will go at once to my father, and say to him, "Father, I have sinned against God and against you. I am no longer fit to be called your son; treat me as one of your hired servants."' If we know ourselves well, we should not have too much difficulty in identifying ourselves with this unfortunate young man, even if we are far from the breadline. I suspect that when our hour of reality dawns, we too will see our lack and deficiency as we prepare for the great transition that we call death.

When the son came within hailing distance of his father's house, the older man ran out to greet him with arms flung around him and passionate kisses. He would hear no apologies or self-denigration on the part of his restored son, but instead prepared a feast to celebrate his homecoming. He clothed him in the best robe, put a ring on his finger, and sandals on his feet. And so the festivities began. Perhaps the most significant part of this welcome, apart from the total acceptance and love of the once-disregarded father (who is a clear image of our heavenly Father), is the son's appreciation of simple gifts that he would once have taken for granted. That meal must have stayed in his memory for the remainder of his life. One of the inevitable results of evil and the suffering it produces is to make us appreciate the apparently simple things of life, such as our health, our home, and family, and our unimpeded access to God in simple worship. Good is, in other words, the obverse side of the coin of experience, whose reverse side is evil. The one cannot be expunged without the other losing its lustre. That much is obvious, even if it is not especially palatable to our sense of moral decency.

All this is made concrete in the appearance of the anti-hero of this parable – the prodigal son's brother: industrious, honest, pious, and any other complimentary moral adjective one may care to add to the list. This brother was furious when he learned the cause of the rejoicing he had heard in the distance, and quite sickened at the invitation to the festive meal. At first he refused to take part in this obvious contravention of justice:

'You know how I have slaved for you all these years; I never once disobeyed your orders; yet you never gave me so much as a kid, to celebrate with my friends. But now that this son of yours turns up, after running through your money with his women, you kill the fatted calf for him' (Luke 15.29–30). How right this criticism is, we feel, for surely the line has to be drawn somewhere! But then we remember the father's defence, and our mood changes, for we suddenly see love in all its radiance trying to reconcile the good and the bad, the righteous and the squalid. ' "My boy", said the father, "you are always with me, and everything I have is yours. How could we fail to celebrate this happy day? Your brother here was dead and has come back to life; he was lost and has been found"' (verses 31–2).

It is the splendid paradox of sin and virtue that the prodigal son had learned to appreciate his father's magnanimity by his open-hearted acceptance of him, sinner as he was, whereas his virtuous brother had a heart as closed as one of stone, noted in Ezekiel 36.26. The promise here was that God would remove such a heart of stone and replace it with a heart of flesh. One does not need much imagination to discern which of the two brothers' hearts was closer to this ideal. There are some people who seem to be naturally kindly disposed to their fellows, but many others have a long journey ahead of them before they even begin to understand the deeper meaning of Amos 5.15: 'Hate evil, and love good; establish justice in the courts; it may be that the Lord, the God of Hosts, will show favour to the survivors of Joseph.' When the establishment of justice is a mark of respect and love for the other person, we have a true knowledge of what is good as opposed to evil, but when justice is followed as a legal routine, it can so easily be contravened, as it was at the time of Amos and the corrupt Kingdom of Israel. The whole edifice has to be smashed before goodness can reassert itself.

The real difficulty with the prodigal son's brother is that he was seeking justice for himself in a situation where he should have been contented, and indeed grateful, that he was not required to undergo the suffering and humiliation of his younger brother. The brother came home a mature man, while he himself had experienced virtually nothing of real life; by this, I do not imply visits to gambling dens, prostitutes, and the like (though there is far worse company that any of these, who at the most ruin only the body). What real living should teach us is the nature of suffering and how best we may serve those who are in pain, the temptations of the flesh and how most effectively we can cope with them, the roots of hatred, both personal and communal, and how best we may relieve those whose lives have been scarred and distorted by prejudices of one type or another that have been hurled at them. The way of real life is inevitably the way of the cross; and few of us can escape tragedy, whether in our own health or in the lives of those especially close to us.

Without the evil of the world, Jesus would have remained respectably alive until he was old and decrepit, but there would have been no resurrection, which was the sign of a new life ahead of all of us who can travel his way of mastery by love and unending service. I suspect that if the prodigal son's brother, like many good religious people (especially of the past), had been confronted with this inventory of horrors contingent on human life day by day, he simply would not have understood. He would have said, quite sincerely, that if you lived decently like him, you would escape all this trouble. Yet what would you have to show for it at the end of the day? A just, virtuous person, yet completely devoid of love, who served his father out of loyalty tinged with more than a little unconscious resentment (did he not speak about 'slaving' in his protest?), who would have been a fine client for a discerning psychotherapist.

This train of thought brings us to the second great parable of Jesus, only five verses long, about the publican (tax-collector) and the Pharisee (Luke 18.9–14). Both met in the temple to pray: the Pharisee was very sure of his great virtue, even to the extent of thanking God that he was not greedy, dishonest, or adulterous like everyone else. Quite the contrary, in fact; he fasted twice a week and paid tithes on all he received. He was especially thankful not to be like the dreadful tax-collector alongside him at prayer; these despised Jews collected taxes for the occupying power, the Romans, and probably extorted money from their fellows because of their powerful position in the community. Yet the tax-collector, in a sudden flash of self-recognition, saw how vile he really was. And so he kept his distance, and would not even raise his eyes to heaven; instead, he beat upon his breast, saying, 'God, have mercy on me, sinner that I am.' God accepted him, just as the father received the prodigal son home with rejoicing. By contrast, the self-righteous Pharisee remained outside the divine love and was not acquitted of his sins in the way the tax-collector was. Let it be understood at once that it was not God who withheld himself from the Pharisee, but the Pharisee who, through his great pride, put up a barrier to a relationship with God. It was the humility of the tax-collector that ensured that he could come to God spontaneously and unreservedly.

In both of these two great parables it is the sinner who is saved, in the context of being healed, while the virtuous man remains in poor spiritual health. No wonder Dame Julian of Norwich was shown that sin is necessary, but that all will be well in the end. And Jesus too came to heal those who were sick, not the healthy. It was the latter who organized his crucifixion, not the former (who, at the most, were unthinking accomplices). What I have been trying to say is that darkness is an integral part of our lives; without it, we would not only fail to appreciate the light, but we would also not grow into mature individuals. The young people who are close to their divine origin that Wordsworth wrote about in his beautiful ode, have in due course to quit the world of distant memory and get started on a constructive passage in this present time and space. The value of the glorious past is that it gives us hope and a degree of guidance for what is to befall us in the future, but we dare not get stuck in it.

Sin is an attitude of mind that shows itself in subsequent action, in which we place what we believe to be our own advantage before that of anyone else; it is a state of radical separation of ourselves from the community as a whole. Yet if we do not give our own welfare priority, we shall perish before the indifference of those around us. It may be that we find ourselves in hospital suffering from a condition that would never have affected us had we paid due attention to our own health. This cannot be good either for us or for society collectively. It would seem that early on in our personal growth we have to take care of our welfare quite selfishly, and that the darkness of the world gives us the strength and resolution to do this. In terms of Jungian psychology, it is the 'shadow' that is fed by the darkness, for it is the place of darkness within the personal and collective unconscious. The shadow brings out the worst in our character, such as lust, jealousy, gluttony, and hatred, which we normally conceal so effectively that we may remain blissfully unaware of what is going on inside our own psyche. Quite often our own friends and associates are less ignorant, for they can discern character traits that show a deeper malaise. How often do racist and sexist prejudices remain latent until a person is in some way thwarted by someone of the despised group! And then the sparks fly. It is not unreasonable to react strongly against an individual provided some sharp practice has been proved. But it can never be right to project our displeasure on to all members of the group to which that person belongs.

It is evident that the shadow is that aspect of the psyche most vulnerable to demonic attack; this shows itself in a capacity to act sinfully. Yet the shadow also provides the psychic energy that is necessary for creative work. At the end of the process of individuation the shadow with its native selfish concern is brought into full relationship with the more elevated functions of the personality, which are concerned with wisdom and service.

In short, I do not find the obvious dark aspects of reality, whether of our individual psyche, of the earth we inhabit, or of the angels around us, a great problem. What we call evil has its creative aspect in our lives no less than what is clearly good. There is no need indeed to posit either a fall in the angelic hierarchy or in human nature. Things are as they are according to the infinitely wise decision of the creator, and we are equally wise to accept things as they are and work accordingly with them. In Voltaire's satire *Candide*, one of the characters, Dr Pangloss, states that this is the best of all possible worlds. On a surface inspection, no contention could be more ridiculous, and this is how it is meant to sound from the lips of that foolish fellow, a parody based on the optimistic philosophy of

Leibniz. Yet on a completely different and much more profound viewing, there is great sense in this contention. God did indeed make everything good, and being a living God, his creation does not end. It continues and will continue until there is a real change in world consciousness, brought about by human initiative (according to Romans 8.18–21; see pages 83–4).

There is nothing especially new in all this, for its basis is found in Isaiah 45.6–7: 'I am the Lord, and there is none other; I make the light, I create the darkness; author alike of wellbeing and woe, I, the Lord, do all these things.' A parallel passage is Deuteronomy 32.39, 'See now that I, I am He, and besides me there is no god: I put to death and I keep alive, I inflict wounds and I heal; there is no rescue from my grasp.' No group has better reason to respond to these words than the Jews, who have suffered abominably in the course of history, but have emerged a people of unprecedented spiritual and mental vigour; and who even today, in greatly diminished numbers as a result of vicious persecution, are still leaders in many of the world's noblest endeavours. Some of their suffering has admittedly followed on their practice of keeping to themselves (at least to some extent) in their worship, but the fruit of this self-imposed isolation is quite refreshing when it is compared with the florid proselytism of some Christian and Muslim groups. The only acceptable conversion is that which follows the demonstration of a better, nobler way, as shown in the lives of the people who subscribe to it. In many religious groups, however, there is a tragically wide divergence between the prescribed way and the lives of its followers. It is hardly surprising that in not a few of the better-educated communities, religious observance is the exception rather than the rule; and yet there is no decrease in the search for God in any community.

From what I have written, it might be supposed that I subscribe to moral relativism, to situation ethics, and that I approve of the permissive society. Nothing in fact could be further from the truth. No one who has been privileged to know mystical illumination (an event I described in an early autobiographical study called *Precarious Living*[2]) could be other than a stern disciplinarian (at least, in their own life). This way of living should prove an example to those close to them, inasmuch as spirituality (the quest for the living God), as opposed to religion (the practice of the way), is caught rather than taught. The angels of darkness may draw us out of the world of comfortable compliance into a wider arena of experience, but in due course their selfish thrust must be counteracted by something that is more altruistic. I recommend for thought the dictum of Hillel, a saintly Pharisee (they were not all bad, despite the Gospel tendency to pillory them *en masse*) who lived shortly before Jesus. The equally saintly Gamaliel (Acts 5.34–9) was his grandson and disciple, and St Paul's teacher (Acts 22.3). Hillel said: 'If I am not for myself, who is for me? If I am only for myself, what am I? If not now, when?' Our first duty is to stay alive and sufficiently well in body and mind so that we are not a burden on society. Our second duty is to give ourselves wholeheartedly to society for the benefit of all its members; and our third duty is expeditiousness – not to put off until tomorrow that which can be done today. The angels of darkness strengthen us, at least to some extent, in the first duty, but it is the angels of light that make our life something more than a morass of selfish desire.

Therefore although by the very nature of our life we are exposed to evil influences, as well as those of a better type that tend towards nobility of character and generosity, we should learn to resist the evil and work in harmony with the good. As Jesus reminds us, 'You will recognize them by their fruit' (Matthew 7.16). This fruit of the Holy Spirit is clearly defined in Galatians 5.22–3: 'But the harvest of the Spirit is love, joy, peace, patience, kindness, goodness, fidelity, gentleness, and self-control.' Paul, a very great mystic, is a stern disciplinarian; before giving this inspiring list of praiseworthy attributes, he warns against the unspiritual gratification of the desires of our bodily nature. His inventory of the types of unspiritual behaviour, which I shall not quote directly because of its length and depressing tone, can be found in Galatians 5.19–21. These are exactly the types of behaviour that are assisted by the angels of darkness working on willing subjects – in other words, people already wracked with envy, anger, or a feeling of crippling impotence as a result of poor self-esteem. This may have followed on from abuse that took place when they were children, and is a potent factor in depressive illness.

As we noted in the last chapter, mentally ill patients are not infrequently attacked by demonic spirits. There is no blame in any of this, for we each have a burden to bear in our life no less than a blessing. Fortunate indeed are they who can see that their burden is their greatest blessing. In other words, our burden nobly borne can bring us into a relationship with many suffering people with whom we can empathize and genuinely help. In the words of Jung, 'Only the wounded surgeon heals.' In the words of Martin Buber, 'All real living is meeting.' To meet, to relate on a deep level of caring, is the real reward of life. I wonder how the brother of the prodigal son would have received this information; only much experience in the common life of humanity would have opened his eyes. Those who suffer do at least have eyes open enough to see, like the man born blind whom Jesus healed (John 9.25).

So is God all light after all? Jung, in his *Answer to Job*, claimed that there was a dark, frankly evil, side to the Deity, no less than a holy one. This view would explain the brutalities of life in no uncertain way. I wonder, though, whether we are entitled to extrapolate the divine nature in terms of human character. I do not object to this as a 'religious' person scandalized by the blasphemy of it all, for to me truth is a crucial ultimate value in the Platonic triad with beauty and goodness, or love. A scientific education has made me wary of all absolute claims, which are certainly tested in the discipline of medical practice. I knew God as love in my earliest childhood, which was not an especially happy one; how could a natural mystic be happy in the company of boisterous children in a milieu in which sport and physical mastery were the qualities most extolled? And remember, I am not blaming anybody, for things are as they are in the world, and no one has the right to alter them according to their own selfish craving.

And yet I knew God as love. I could not have loved a capricious tyrant who was half, or even quarter, evil and cruel, for I would never have known where I stood with him. I would have trembled before him as I did before some schoolteachers who were particularly sarcastic; I would have obeyed, but there would have been no love. This love enables one to flow out in unreserved compassion to all that lives, and to give up one's very life as a sacrifice in the way that Jesus did. As a youngster, I could not have put all my feelings into this type of theological language, but my heart was in the right place in all important issues – of which the treatment of the black population was the most outstanding. (I spent my youth in South Africa.) Therefore I continue to hold that God is light, and in him there is no darkness at all.

The love of which I speak is no sentimental outpouring of effusive sympathy that does little to share the burden or relieve the pain. It is, on the contrary, the very power that enables growth to take place even in the midst of terrible suffering. Proverbs 3.11–12 has it well measured, 'My son, do not spurn the Lord's correction or recoil from his reproof; for those whom the Lord loves he reproves, and he punishes the son who is dear to him.' This reproof may follow in the wake of some misdemeanour, but it may also be part of the spiritual training God has in store for the elect – those who have spontaneously elected to be God's servants just as Hannah entered her young son Samuel into God's service at Shiloh (1 Samuel 1.26–8). Samuel's subsequent career fully justified Hannah's undertaking. Job's sufferings were under the full aegis of God, though executed by Satan, who is depicted as a member of the court of heaven and who ranges over the earth from end to end (Job 1.6–7). The darkest love of God encompassed Jesus crucified on the cross of human malice and cruelty; it found its release and fulfilment on the third day when Jesus revealed himself to his friends in his new resurrection body. Therefore although there is indeed an element of dark suffering in God's relationship with us through Jesus Christ, the source of the pain is the pure love of God that reveals itself in uncreated light. God may have created darkness for our learning of various basic social issues, but in the end all this is to be raised up to God for a final blessing.

In Chapter 4 I quoted Origen as saying that all men are moved by two angels: an evil one who inclines them to evil, and a good one who inclines them to good. He attributed good or evil thoughts directly to these guardian spirits, but today

95

we would see the matter primarily to be one of temperament and environment, which I believe to be more accurate than Origen's assessment of human behaviour. Yet I would not discard the concept of these two angels as being influencing agents in our lives. I have tried to show that both have their place, and that the evil one need not be summarily decried and expelled. We simply do not understand the full meaning and purpose of life sufficiently to dismiss or expel anything of a spiritual nature, any more than Peter could call unclean any food that God had made in the sequence of events that led up to Cornelius' reception into the Christian community (Acts 10.15).

Nevertheless, in my own deliverance work, I command any demonic spirits to leave their present situation where they are causing trouble, and I direct them with love 'to that place in the life beyond death which God has prepared for their reception and healing'. I remember that they are as much children of God as I am, and it is not for me to become imperious in my instructions. Instead, I regard it as an indescribably great privilege to do this work, and I look for the time when all the dark angels will have done their essential work, and will be ready to depart finally to the divine protection and love where no doubt more will be shown them, as it is also shown to us when we make the great transition that we call death.

In my deliverance work I have also been 'instructed' (by unseen teachers of great wisdom) to 'free the spirits from all obedience to evil humanity'. This stresses how powerful humans can be in the propagation of evil, and can actually enslave angels. The type of approach that attributes most of our human delinquencies to demonic influence is certainly far off the mark. A violent crime may be precipitated by demonic influence, but the tendency would be already fully at work in the perpetrator of the crime, who would therefore be justly accountable for his or her actions in a court of law. In the same way, it is unsatisfactory, to say the least, to blame the crimes committed by Hitler and his associates on demonic attacks made against them. Personally, I believe that Hitler was a great medium for the dark forces, yet his total responsibility remains. One hopes that he too is learning about love and forgiveness in a more understanding milieu on the other side of life.

So is there no end to the angels of darkness? Will the demons be with us for ever? God alone knows the answer to such a profound question, but such thoughts are never far from the surface of my mind. At one time, conflicts were resolved by warfare, and the victor subjugated the vanquished to a variable degree of ignominy and humiliation. In the conquest of Canaan by Joshua and the Israelites, only a complete destruction of Jericho and Ai would suffice. Today, all but some belligerent fundamentalists regard such episodes with distaste bordering on shame. They certainly show God in a quite unacceptable light. On a more secular level, the days of conquest by warfare are also drawing to a welcome close. At the end of the First World War, which claimed the lives of millions of fine young men, Germany was smashed and humiliated by France, Britain, and the United States among others. We all know the history of the German revival under Hitler: the Germans were a great but proud people who could not bear the humiliation of defeat, and the great financial depression of the late 1920s served to incapacitate any alternative government. The Germans were all set on revenge, and apart from their punitive action against the Jews, they spread insidiously over Central Europe until a further piece of aggression against Poland made the Second World War inevitable. The bestial cruelty of the Germans who overran much of Europe, including France and Western Russia, is something that even today beggars description, but six years later they and their equally cruel Japanese allies were roundly defeated by the combined might of Russia, the United States, and Britain. This time it was the civilians who suffered the most casualties (apart from the cruelty of Germany and Japan), through air attacks that culminated in the destruction of Dresden and the explosion of nuclear bombs on Hiroshima and Nagasaki in Japan.

This time, though, the victors had learned an important lesson: there are no lasting victories in war. The sequel of the previous war taught them this piece of wisdom, and so both Germany and Japan were treated kindly (admittedly Germany was partitioned with a communist eastern portion under Russian control, but this was a political arrangement and not a punitive one), despite the horrors they had committed. Today both countries play an important role in the financial stability of the entire world, and are largely focuses of equity and tolerance.

The same approach to spiritual matters seems to be right: good has to flow out in love towards evil, and encompass it with the power of the Holy Spirit. In such an intimate relationship of self-giving, God will enter the darkness and illuminate it fully, not with the earthly light of peace and harmony alone, but also with the uncreated light of his presence, that same light that we considered in Chapter I in relation to mystical experience. For God is indeed light, and in him there is no darkness at all. When the darkness and the light of the world come together in the divine presence, both are transmuted and brought into the glory of the uncreated light from which they originally sprang, and to which they are to return, bringing the whole created universe with them. Then indeed God in Christ will be all, and be in all, not merely as a theological statement (Colossians 3.11), but as a fact of existence.

The greatest mystics have had no compunction in describing God as beyond good and evil, because both these categories are limited to human understanding. We have seen how 'good' people like the brother of the prodigal son and the Pharisee in both these famous parables may be further removed from the love of God than decidedly 'bad' profligates and tax-collectors, who on the surface seem to be quite disgraceful specimens of personhood. The 'good', zealous members of religious groups not infrequently tend to persecute those of whom they disapprove, whereas the 'bad', indifferent ones at least have the courtesy to leave them alone – a few may even be warm-hearted enough to take them under their wing, for there is not infrequently a fellow-feeling among those who have few illusions about their frailty. By contrast, the self-righteous are seldom blessed with hearts of flesh.

It is noteworthy that Jesus himself demurred at being called 'good' by the stranger, usually identified as a rich young man, who asked instructions for winning the prize of eternal life (Mark 10.18). Jesus answered that no one is good except God alone. I cannot believe that Jesus had a guilty conscience, for I could not imagine a better person than he. I think that what he meant was this: in this world of duality between good and evil, no one can be completely uncontaminated by evil no matter how fine a person they may be, for it clings to one like dirt. If Jesus had not been thus afflicted, he would not have partaken of the usual human condition, and therefore his humanity would have been special and unlike that of the general run of humankind. The judgement depends on what Jesus did with this clinging evil: whether he succumbed to its presence and committed sinful actions, or whether he ignored it and went on his way doing good. In his case, we know the answer.

Describing God as beyond good and evil does not mean that these categories are not significant to us and that a self-styled 'spiritual' person is no longer subject to the moral law, a situation called antinomianism. God is indeed good, as Jesus said to his enquirer, but the divine nature is so superlatively good that it beggars all human categories of goodness. It is so intense that it can embrace evil into itself and convert it into good by the power of love. Therefore the highest goodness is love; and God *is* love, as we read in 1 John 4.8 and 4.16. He showed his love by sending his only Son into the world that we might have life through him; furthermore, he who dwells in love is dwelling in God, and God in him. True love is universal in scope; if humans can love even a few of their fellows, they are doing well. The essence of love is the giving of oneself for another's benefit in order that they may attain something of what God has in mind for them. What this may be is not one's business, lest one gets in the way by imposing one's own will and views of them, and distorting the way ahead.

To end on a practical note, evil actions are not to be tolerated. The evil-doer, perhaps a criminal, should be apprehended as soon as possible – as much for their own good as the safety of society. It is best to come to terms with one's delinquencies as soon as possible in order to embark on a better way of life at once. Every action has its reaction; God is not fooled, for as we sow, so we shall reap (Galatians 6.7). But once there has been a candid admission of sin, the punishment should be constructive rather than merely painful and humiliating; to be found out is enough humiliation for the normal person. Where the evil-doer is clearly mentally deranged, the appropriate psychiatric measures should be instituted. As I have already indicated, there may be a place for a deliverance ministry also. Just as demonic spirits are sent to God's care, so should evil people be brought to God in prayer, and their welfare attended to by the social arm of the community. Prayer is our essential link with God, being the way of connection between us both. God initiates the prayer, and we transmit the power of the Holy Spirit to those for whom we intercede. I have little doubt that the angels of light play a vital part in this work.

The same principles hold true for the world situation. While a generalized global conflict is less likely now that peace has been restored among the major powers, there is still enough savage warfare in other countries to make the ideal of 'Glory to God in highest heaven, and on earth peace to all in whom he delights' (Luke 2.14), sung by the angels at the time of the nativity, a long way off. It is interesting and ironical that the armed forces of the major powers are employed not for national expansion, but for peace-keeping duties in the various trouble spots of the world.

The question arises: what is the real difference between an angel of light and one of darkness? My own view is that the dark angel has a limited understanding of its place in the cosmos – in fact, is hardly able to see beyond its own being. The angel of light has a truly cosmic vision, and can function far beyond its own apparent situation. In other words, a dark angel is virtually blind, its vision being restricted to its milieu that it guards selfishly and with little regard to the benefit of anything else. Yet its divine origin ensures that it cannot cause irreparable damage, because at the end of the day it is a creature of light. The basis of angelic darkness is ignorance rather than ill will. Indeed, it could be argued that ignorance is the basis of human sin also: if only we knew the reality of life and stopped grasping after things of one type or another, we would not only know enduring happiness, but would also start to give happiness to everyone else. Unfortunately, sin that starts as childish ignorance can soon escalate through avarice and sordid rivalry to destructive hatred and a capacity to kill all who stand in the way of the human predator. I do not see the angel of darkness pursuing this course, even if it can aggravate human wickedness.

The degree of free will that an angel possesses is limited, whereas human free will is of impressive range and potency; no wonder the human has a greater prospect for development than an angel (see Chapter 1). So why are some humans saintly and others bestial? We may find a scientific explanation for variations in human behaviour, but these do not answer the fundamental question; they merely state it in another form. St Paul wrestles with this question in Romans 9.6–22 with special reference to 'Jacob I loved and Esau I hated' (from Malachi 1.2–3). The hatred that the prophet attributes to God is clearly in direct opposition to the unconditional love God has for all his creatures. If, however, the creature transgresses the law of life, expressed both in the Bible and in the common run of civil responsibility, suffering even to death is likely to be a consequence. It is this that appears superficially to be God's displeasure. The question remains: why do people vary so much in their moral obedience? Paul comes to the conclusion that the potter cannot be held to account if the pot he fashioned is imperfect. The fact indeed that he tolerates such a bad product is evidence of his mercy; Paul is thinking of unconverted Jews in this context, which becomes quite savage as the chapter reaches its end. Nowadays this type of attitude to the non-Christian Jews is quite unacceptable, and indeed Paul himself becomes less severe in his later Letter to the Ephesians. He has come to see that Christ is already exalted, the ruler of the cosmos, and his presence as universal lord ensures the unity of Jews and Gentiles, who are now reconciled since each is equally part of the new humanity and advance together towards the Father (Ephesians 2.11–22). This understanding of Christ as already exalted over the entire creation is called the 'realized eschatology', and is characteristic of Paul's Letters to the Colossians and the Ephesians.

This great efflorescence of Pauline mystical genius could well be the solution of the problem about the gross moral inequalities inherent in human nature. In our own ignorance we may have to undergo many adventures, some of enormous suffering, before we, like the prodigal son, learn better cosmic manners. Even in the course of our life on earth we can learn a great deal, especially if we are in good mental health, but

8

The Teaching Quality of Angels

❖❖❖

The word 'angel' is derived from the Greek *angelos*, the Hebrew counterpart of which is *malakh*, which is translated as 'messenger'. The last book of the Old Testament is called Malachi, which means 'my messenger'. Whether this was the actual name of the writer or simply a cognomen one does not know. Yet one thing is certain: the Book of Malachi contains a grave message to the newly settled exiles from Babylon who have now returned to the Holy Land (a term for Palestine first found in the earlier Book of Zechariah), and have again forgotten the precept of the Law by failing in their religious duties and by the scandal of mixed marriages and divorce. Malachi also says there will come a day when God will purify the priesthood, destroy the wicked, and secure the triumph of righteousness. There is also a beautiful consoling oracle, 'Bring the whole tithe into the treasury; let there be food in my house. Put me to the proof, says the Lord of Hosts, and see if I do not open windows in the sky and pour a blessing on you as long as there is need' (Malachi 3.10).

The messenger of light brings tidings from God; and it is quite probable that the prophets of Israel were inspired by angels of light who brought the power of the Holy Spirit to them (see Chapter 4). Angelic messages of instruction on a highly moral level can occur in the lives of lesser mortals also. I have been the instrument of angelic instruction throughout my ministry in the Church of God, which is the world at large no less than a place of denominational worship. It is good to know that God has no religion, but is involved in all religions; we remember St Paul's injunction, '... all that is true, all that is noble, all that is just and pure, all that is lovable and attractive, whatever is excellent and admirable – fill your thoughts with these things' (Philippians 4.8). The Spirit of

God is not merely in these things, but is the inspiration behind them. Where a religion reveals these qualities, God's presence is not too far away. On the other hand, where there is falsehood and evil, the angels of darkness congregate; in fact, no religion is free from this taint. However, its very presence tends to stimulate the powers of light to perform their work of transformation: nothing evokes the power of light more radically than an obfuscating darkness. It is thus that humanity can undergo the growth that follows the interaction of the angels of darkness and those of light. We considered this paradoxical state of affairs in the last chapter. God looks for something more than virtue; he desires a transformed humanity made into something of the image of Christ. The essential key is always love.

A close friend of mine, whose life has not been an easy one, has been kind enough to write out the following encounter with an angel of light, who showed him a great deal about the nature of worldly success, truth, and integrity. This man, now in his forties, is widely read in world religions and an authority in Jungian studies. Yet despite this, he has not been able to gain a foothold on the rungs of the academic ladder:

> For a brief time in the late 1980s, I had more confidence in the future. In the autumn of 1988, I had established contact with the head of a department of a well-established provincial university, and found someone in academia who spoke the same language as I did. After our meeting it seemed only logical that I should embark on a programme of doctoral research. Of course, there were no funds for this and I would have to finance myself by means of supply teaching; but it seemed faint-hearted not to take up this opportunity. Moreover, if I could keep going for the first year and produce some high-quality work, I could then apply for a grant or scholarship with the backing of the university.
>
> When I began the course in the spring of the following year, there was no reason to doubt the wisdom of my decision. I found my superior stimulating, and enjoyed his style of trenchant criticism. A letter to a distinguished Jungian analyst requesting a slot in a depth-psychology journal for

my first research paper had elicited a positive response, and this gave an added impetus. However, as the year progressed I began to see the writing on the wall! First, I was dismayed to learn that this university does not give a damn about its graduates. There was no chance of any backing from this source, although it could be relied on to raise the cost of my tuition fees by £100 each year. I then discovered that my superior was in a somewhat marginal position in the order of things. By way of defence, he resorted to frantic overwork and an obsessive preoccupation with academic politics. As the pressures on him mounted, so the quality of his supervision deteriorated.

If the government's ill-conceived plans for reform of the universities were taking their toll on my supervisor, the equally abortive plans for the schools were undermining me. Supply teaching is precarious and stressful work at the best of times; now it was becoming intolerable. I needed a research grant as a matter of urgency, but this had proved to be a remote and elusive possibility. After some bids that inevitably came to nothing, I could see no other option but to discontinue the doctorate. I took an intermission for 1989–90 in the hope that circumstances would be more favourable for the next academic year.

Fate was not in a benevolent mood in 1990. The pressures of the classroom intensified, and so did a low-level migraine I acquired early in that year. At the same time, my marriage was under strain, and our housing situation was unsatisfactory to say the least. By October 1990, the container was on the verge of collapse. What was I to do to halt or reverse this alarming state of affairs? There was perhaps one option. If I could secure a research fellowship from Oxford or Cambridge, this would transform the socio-economic situation that was undermining my health and marriage, it would save my research project, and restore our shattered confidence in the future. However, everything rested on a big 'if'. I knew that competition for such fellowships is ferocious, and I would be one of forty applicants. Yet even if I had only a 1 per cent chance of success, was this not worth taking? The alternative seemed unthinkable – or so I reasoned with my ego.

Despite all the pressure and disruption, I managed to put together some passable research proposals for a fellowship at one of the Cambridge colleges. Once I had sent it off, I could only wait for the date in mid-December when the short-listed candidates would be notified. As the splitting apart continued unabated, I increasingly pinned my hopes on this 1 per cent chance.

The angelic intervention must have occurred in the first or second week in December, close to the eagerly awaited deadline. I had not slept well that night, and was wide awake in the early hours of the morning (3.00–4.00 a.m.); my wife was fast asleep. I sensed a presence above me in the top right-hand corner of the room. I remained on my back and focused my gaze at an angle of 60 degrees. The presence took no perceptible form, and communicated with me by direct intuition. My thoughts then translated the intuition into words, so that I was having an intrapsychic dialogue with an extrapsychic presence.

I was asked if I wanted the fellowship for its own sake or as a means of extricating myself from my predicament. Naturally I wanted to give an unconditional 'yes', as the question implied that the fellowship could be mine if I really wanted it. Despite my commitment to pursuing my research by any means possible, I hesitated. This was not on account of my misgivings about joining the establishment – it was rather that I was not sure that I wanted to be let off the hook in this way. My ongoing confrontation with adverse fate or the dark face of God was, presumably, an essential part of my individuation. I felt that if I did not see it through, I would be irrevocably diminished – in short, a Cambridge fellow.

After I admitted to my inability to give my assent, the presence remained for a little while. I felt the awkwardness of being at a loss for words before a person of immense authority. This was numinous unworth of a kind, but also abasement on account of what my ego had put me up to.

In the face of such transpersonal authority, I felt slightly ridiculous.

The Cambridge college declined to put me on the short-list for their fellowship; and after two more intermission years, I withdrew completely from the doctoral programme of the provincial university.

My friend continues on the precarious course of supply teaching, but is growing spiritually by the day. No longer set on conquering the world of professional studies, he is able to set his mind to considering some of the deeper mysteries of our life in the shadow of God's presence. His wife, fortunately, is solidly behind his endeavours, but there are no children – no doubt a blessing when one considers his way of living. He has no affiliation with any religious group because no one religion could encompass the scope of his spirituality. This is a pity not so much for him as for the religious community, for he has much to offer.

Another friend who has had a useful teaching visit from angels is a middle-aged lady with grown-up daughters, but who looks very youthful. She is a practising Christian of growing spirituality and wide sympathies. Here is her very recent story:

Last night I developed symptoms and felt ill. There is illness at work at present, lasting a number of days. This morning I experienced a bad head, dry throat, sickness, etc. I knew it was going to be bad, so prepared myself as best I could. I came home at lunch-time, did what was necessary, and went to bed. I switched the TV on, although my eyes really couldn't stand the movement. It was the story of an Indian tribe who had captured a white couple and their baby. The woman was telling the Indians the nativity story; I then turned the TV off. Quite some time later, I turned it on again. She was saying about the angel visiting Mary and how she was filled with the Holy Spirit. This passage had been coming to me in many different ways. I did think how extraordinary that all this should happen at the flick of a switch. The reason I am writing this is because all my symptoms disappeared, though I had previously been feeling so groggy. I decided that if after some time this really had happened, I would write to you. I am certainly experiencing things outside my control, feeling helpless in the situation, but things seem to be all right. I still can't quite believe it, but I am feeling better.

In this much simpler account than that of the supply teacher, it would seem that the angels and the Holy Spirit were working together to heal the woman of an influenza-like illness and, more important, to bring her to a greater spiritual awareness. She had no idea that I was in the process of writing a book about angels, but was delighted that her small experience should be used as I wished it. However, the matter did not end there. In her next letter she wrote:

I wasn't completely cured. The symptoms I described to you didn't come back, but four days later (Tuesday, 27th), knowing I was going back to work on the 28th, I went out to a church service and got worse and worse on my return. I had a severe headache, and all the symptoms of a head cold came out. All this meant a re-run with the practice manager over the phone, and discussing when I would be back at work. I had to hold on to the fact that things had improved [in her work in the medical practice], and keep that uppermost in my mind.

Previously I hadn't been to the doctor, and the practice manager kept asking why I hadn't gone. I'm sure she didn't believe I was ill. This time I've imagined the next day I'll be fine, but the next day proved me wrong. In the end I went to my doctor, and she told me to take the week off. As much as anything, I think my sinuses are blocked.

All along, whatever has happened to me I do feel has been meant. It was a tremendous hurdle to come through with the practice manager, and thankfully the atmosphere was fine, the doctor taking the stress out of the situation in the end.

What is, to my mind, especially noteworthy about this simple account of spiritual experience is the gradually expanding field of awareness. It would have sounded much more satisfying to have announced a complete, lasting recovery at the end of the television viewing, but, no, after a period of remission there was a recrudescence of illness that found its end in an atmosphere, previously lacking, of harmony in the medical practice in which my friend plays a valuable part as full-time receptionist. I can just imagine how helpful her presence is to the various patients, making them feel fully at home. Any type of loving work is best performed when one knows what it feels like to be out in the cold – perhaps after a broken marriage or a severe illness. A real healing is more than a merely personal affair, for it brings in other people also.

For some considerable number of years, there has been the phenomenon of people, either in trance or in apparently normal consciousness, bringing through teaching what purports to be a source of intelligence higher than the ordinary human mind with its store of knowledge. This process is called *channelling*, and the person who transmits the teaching may or may not be entirely cognizant of what is being transmitted through them. Often the credentials of the source of information remain obscure, even if a definite name is supplied. There is clearly a relationship between channelling and spiritualistic mediumship, and also 'New Age' metaphysic; but, as we noted in Chapter 5, some communicators give important, indeed urgent, advice about the state of the world that cannot be faulted for the gravity of its message. Much such teaching is geared at people who are initiated into more expansive ways of thought. This is what is meant by esoteric doctrine, but some of this is arrogant and irritatingly self-assured (as are some dogmatic religious teachings from all the world faiths when placed in the hands of basically insecure people who need to assert themselves to prove their authority). Not all higher spiritual teaching need have an unpleasant esotericism; some of it is simple and direct, so that the disciples can attain a finer knowledge by a simple awareness of the present moment. One thinks here of the spiritual teaching present in the Gospels, the Hebrew prophets, and much of the scriptures of the other world faiths.

A relatively recent book brings in esoteric teaching on a

much more simple, practical level. It is called *Talking with Angels*[1], and consists of protocols and notes that describe actual events that took place in Hungary during 1943 and 1944, when the country was under German domination, but was for a time free of actual occupation. Four people were involved, three were Jews called Hanna, Joseph (her husband), and Lili, and one was a Gentile called Gitta. Ultimately Gitta Mallasz alone survived, since she was only peripherally involved in the Holocaust (she suffered for sheltering Jewish women), while the others were all killed in concentration camps. From June 1943 until November 1944, Hanna received communications from the life beyond death, but the teaching was distinctly different from the usual 'New Age' material that is so widely current. There were eighty-eight 'dialogues' altogether, initially addressed to Hanna, Lili, and occasionally Joseph, but towards the end the teaching was general, because the individuals were scattered and increasingly in danger of persecution and death.

Gitta Mallasz was eventually able to emigrate to France, taking the written material that she transcribed from Hanna's addresses. This material formed the basis of the book written in French and translated into German and English. In his fine preface, the English translator Robert Hinshaw commends the work's straightforward, down-to-earth character, in contrast to so many publications dealing with esoteric matters. He also comments on the naturalness with which these four 'ordinary' young people, none of whom had ever had significant religious instruction, accepted the sudden appearance of 'angels' into their everyday existence: it shows that possibilities for new ways and for transformation do come to us when there seems to be no way out, if only we are open to them; for, as Hinshaw observes, this luminous and numinous event came to the four just at the darkest hour of their lives.

The earliest dialogues are not especially arresting, except for those to whom they were addressed. Awareness, especially of their own disposition and its ambivalent nature, is stressed, and Gitta and Lili are encouraged to question the communicator about what has been said as well as their own personal problems. Joseph played only a very small part in the proceedings. In the course of the fifth dialogue, Gitta states that her dearest desire is to serve, and she is told that her task is mighty and wondrous. The vibration of these words spoken through Hanna conveys to Gitta a foretaste of a completely new life intensity. Behind the spoken words, she sensed an infinite multitude in perfect harmony, and she wondered whether her 'teacher' could be what we humans call an 'angel'. With lowered eyes and upward-turned hands, the following words are gently spoken by her 'teacher': 'We sing praise, we praise the Divine.' When Gitta asks whether they always see God, she is told, 'You know not what you say. Ask another question.'

In the thirteenth dialogue, Gitta experiences a remarkable baptism with what appears to be blue water. Hanna requires some water to drink during her arduous work, but then Gitta is told to drink. With astonishment, she obeys. Through the eyes of Gitta's angel, Hanna sees blue light reflected in the water. As she drinks she has the impression that this blue light is streaming throughout her body, even into the finest blood vessels. Her angel then says to her, 'When you are hard inside, when something is blocked in your heart, remember this water. It dissolves everything. Do you feel it?' She feels wonderful, believing that this must be divine grace. The angel says, 'You give me water from *below*. I give you water from *above*. Give to all who thirst, and the water from *above* will always flow. It is to the Divine that you give every drop.' This dialogue illustrates the high spirituality of the teaching.

In the fourteenth dialogue, Gitta asks what true humility is. Her angel tells her that it is easy to recognize: 'If you bow your head and feel uplifted – this is *true humility*. If you bow your head and feel lowered – this is *false humility*.' In the sixteenth dialogue, we find the interesting dictum, 'For the strong, sin is a lesson. For the weak, it is damnation.' A crucial part of the teaching, first outlined in the nineteenth dialogue, is that the human's great task is to bridge the abyss between the created world of mineral, plant, and animal and the creating world of angels. There are seven levels, or centres, of which the human is the fourth. Much later on, in the forty-fourth dialogue, the creating world is shown to extend beyond the angel (symbolizing peace and silence) to the seraph (symbolizing pure joy and shining power) and a seventh level, which is called the mysterious, the highest degree of all life. In the sixty-third dialogue, this mysterious being is finally identified as the Son of God. In this dialogue, there is the interesting teaching about baptism: the Son of God on the wooden cross; beginning and end, earth and heaven – the first baptism. The second baptism is water baptism: union of water and joy (the connection of the plant and the seraph). The third baptism is baptism by fire: harmony united with silence, movement and peace (the connection of the animal and the angel). Thus the original six levels are contracted into three. The fourth, or human, level remains unattached in the middle, and is the means of final union of Creator and creation: there are no longer seven levels, but one alone. It is no wonder that the Word became flesh and made his home among us (John 1.14).

I could continue quoting memorable practical spiritual teaching, but what has been given should illustrate the general tenor of *Talking with Angels*. Early on, God is only occasionally mentioned, and Christ's name even less so. In the concluding pages, though, all is concentrated on Christ, and the impression produced is a particularly acceptable one, distinctly different from the usual religious stereotype that tends to deaden one's full response to him and all he stands for in our disordered world. The angels do not look for very virtuous people treading the same paths as in the past, but a new person completely. Towards the end of the Second World War, many spiritually minded people thought along similar lines (one recalls Dietrich Bonhoeffer's *Letters and Papers from Prison*). The angels were emphatic in predicting that a new order of living was not far away, but over fifty years have elapsed since they communicated with their gallant band of disciples, and the degree of spiritual progress among humans has been negligible. Perhaps the 'new order' will be concurrent with the parousia, Christ's second coming in the world.

It is not without significance that the impressive teaching outlined in *Talking with Angels* was transmitted by a young Jewish woman who knew little about the Christian religion, or probably any other religion either. Both Hanna and Gitta were artists, and worked quite closely together later in their lives. Hanna's husband Joseph was a furniture designer, and Lili gave courses in bodily movement therapy. Once the German army invaded Hungary, the full force of anti-Jewish destruction broke loose. Hanna and Lili could have escaped, having been persuaded to become baptized in order to present themselves as Christians. They demurred, considering the action as opportunistic, but Gitta saw otherwise. The earlier baptism with the 'blue water' had produced a lasting effect on her, so that she was able to see that the sacraments are symbols of an inner process: a spiritual reality might act through a corresponding spiritual form, a thought that occurs at the end of the sixty-second dialogue. Be this as it may, in the end Hanna and Lili openly revealed their Jewish origin to the German SS guards, although Hanna looked conspicuously 'Aryan' with her fair complexion and straight nose, and could easily have passed herself off as a gentile Hungarian. Instead, she and Lili died nobly in a concentration camp, as did Joseph (in another concentration camp) at almost the same time.

The book needs to be read slowly and meditatively. The first pages may seem to drag, but the angelic teacher knew how necessary it is to start with basic discussions about purpose and motive. As the book unfolds, so its exceptional spiritual authority becomes evident; the angels had certainly performed a considerable work.

Another kind friend has given me an account of a fairly typical angelic experience that also has a teaching component. She writes:

During the Second World War a colleague and I had been evacuated to Burford (in Oxfordshire), and one hot Sunday we set off for a cycle ride. All road signs had been removed, in fear of an invasion, but my friend knew the way and we cycled for several miles until a lowering cloud burst suddenly and rain sheeted down. My friend, then in front, called over her shoulder, but the words were drowned and I soared past her downhill as the road grew ever steeper. I pulled hard on the brakes with no response, and at terrifying speed I saw the horrifically steepening road veering sharply to the left, with a tall Cotswold drystone wall, with its blocks of bumpy stone, confronting it. I had instantly to choose between heading straight at the wall or turning left downhill and being squashed against it. I rode straight *at* the wall, and with a terrific impact lost consciousness for several moments ... I came to sitting astride the top of the wall; and whereas I had, seconds before, been sitting on my cycle, now the cycle was sitting on me, across the back of my neck (I can't begin to fathom how), the wheels whizzing madly round, one each side of my shoulders.

I felt no weight, I felt no pain, and in my shocked state I was conscious of one thing only: two angels appeared in the air in front of me, a little to the left – mighty Presences, ten feet high, just shapes, with wings, no details – but laughing and laughing at the neat way they had fielded me.

They vanished (and after that I could recall only isolated shots): slowly I felt a dislocated little finger, a flayed inch of skin above one knee – no more, no pain, just shock. Then my friend appeared, wheeling her bicycle slowly downhill; a man drove up in a car; my glasses had flown off, to land unhurt upon a thistle; of my collapsing from the bottom of the wall and insisting on lying down on the soaking verge under the pelting rain to recover; of a moment in the car; of entering a cottage with a sofa opposite the front door and being helped invisibly towards it; and last, my neck and shoulders miraculously untouched and of mounting my completely undamaged, unbuckled, unpunctured, unscathed bicycle in the sunshine, and riding all the way home.

Angels had never meant anything to me till then (though I had never been so near to death): they lived only in the past. Now they saved and strengthened me for the suffering that loomed two months ahead.

The young lady entered a convent some two months after the events recorded above, but was rejected three years later, with even greater suffering, for her 'vocation' had seemed so powerful. She realized that she was to share in the sufferings of Jesus, rejected by his fellow-Jews. The words 'Go, for I will send you to the Gentiles far away' sparked off her subsequent life of service in the world. She was taught much about the relative nature of all material appearances in her experience of a miracle superintended by angels. But then came the disappointment, followed by a completely different life of service.

Another rather different type of miracle mediated by angelic agencies occurred in the life of this woman about ten years later:

A nun in a contemplative community wrote urgently asking if I could place this quotation from Browning:

> Religion's all or nothing; it's no mere smile
> of contentment, sigh of aspiration, sir . . .

She badly wanted it for a talk she was about to give to the Mothers' Union. It required an immediate answer, but I could not remember ever meeting the words. I opened at random my Browning volume of 696 pages in double columns and small print with sadness in my plea for help, knowing I had no time to search.

The first two lines I saw* were those she had sent – a miraculous answer to her habitual, adaptable prayer when in need, i.e. 'Lord, I *need* this quotation. Please take possession of my thinking so that I may search in the right place; or please send my guardian angel to show my dear friend where to look.'

Yet how does one discern an angelic message from that of an impostor? The answer lies in Jesus' criterion, 'You will recognize them by their fruit' (Matthew 7.16, 20). A dubious spirit tends to boost the ego, making the person feel superior to others, while a genuine angelic encounter lights up the whole being of the person with faith, hope, and love.

In 1 John 4.1–3, we are warned not to trust every spirit, but to test the spirits to see whether they come from God. The way of discernment that is recommended is to ascertain that the spirit acknowledges that Jesus Christ has come in the

---

* The lines are from *Mr Sludge, 'The Medium'*, a very long, minor work that I had never read.

flesh; if it does so, it is indeed from God. Of course making such a verbal confession of faith is not beyond the wiles of Satan. As the saying goes, 'actions speak louder than words'. If the spirit leads one to a finer way of life, less ego-centred and more self-giving to others, the Spirit of Christ is indeed with one. If on the other hand, one's religion makes one exclusive in one's attitude and destructively critical of other people, one should beware. This was not the way of Jesus, who had no difficulty in mixing with many different types of people. He may have dissented radically from some of their opinions, but I do not see him ever withdrawing his love from anyone, no matter how depraved their lifestyle or how cruel their behaviour to humans or animals. Acceptance at least bears the possibility of redemption of the offender from the bondage of evil attitudes, whereas rejection does no one any good. Of course, intractably stubborn behaviour inevitably brings with it a heavy quota of disapproval, which quite reasonably can culminate in total rejection until there is repentance. The law of social responsibility as laid down in the Bible is not disregarded lightly, but fortunately there is forgiveness once an honest attempt at an amended life has been ventured.

When one considers these accounts of a few individuals' experiences of angels, a certain pattern emerges. They were all spiritually uplifting because the recipients were caring people who did not stint themselves in their work for others. Whereas the supply teacher is someone of superb intellect, the lady who works as a receptionist in a medical practice would claim no special mental capacity, but through the vicissitudes of her life she has gained a considerable degree of practical wisdom in organizing her domestic affairs, so that at present she is of great help to a number of people. It is worth distinguishing between learning, of which the receptionist has little, and wisdom, in which she is growing. Learning follows the direct application of the rational mind to acquiring knowledge, and as such is invaluable in doing the intellectual work set before us. Wisdom, however, is an overall view of existence whereby we can live as profitably with nature and as harmoniously with our fellow creatures as possible. Learning finds its apogee when the mind confronts the great mysteries of life, and by various philosophies attempts to reach a conclusion. As we noted at the beginning of the book, thought will never give us the final answer; love alone suffices, for by love we come to the full unitive knowledge of God, who is the source of all wisdom. Angels are creatures of God's wisdom that come to us when we are ready to receive them. The learning of the supply teacher needed to be obfuscated before angelic wisdom could approach him. By contrast the much humbler mental capacity of the receptionist was able to receive angelic communication of a very much more basic type, one that simply encouraged her in the daily round of her existence.

In the instance of the young lady who had her miraculous brush with death only to emerge virtually unscathed from the encounter, one can envisage her character quite clearly: a clean-living, religious person hoping to enter a contemplative community. Her spirituality was full of vigour, so that she could enjoy the beauties of nature and the full use of her body in cycling down country lanes during the Second World War. When the inevitability of an accident stared her in the face, she calmly decided on a clear course of action and then remained still. Somehow she had tuned into the rhythm of the cosmos, so that aid from sources far beyond intellectual understanding was available to her. She was privileged to see the angels who ministered this aid that came from God himself. Her mind was free of guile and distractions, so she was open to the divine grace. In the second episode, when she was able to find an obscure quotation from Browning merely by opening a large book at the right place, she was receptive to the direct inspiration of her guardian angel.

These three people all share a common concern with spiritual matters. None would think much of themselves, but all would agree that the quest for God is the most important consideration in their life. I feel sure that the same point of view would have been affirmed by the four Hungarians who were involved in writing *Talking with Angels*. When people of more mundane interests, those who would not normally care very much about God except perhaps in a customary institutional way, encounter an angel, there has nearly always been some crisis in their lives that knocks them off their perch of worldly assurance. This brings them into contact with a source of wisdom far exceeding anything that the world has to offer. It is not surprising that after an angelic encounter the person feels much better in body as well as mind. I wonder whether the Hungarian group would have been able to do their important work had their country not been in the greatest danger and their own lives in growing peril.

It is interesting finally to consider the criteria that St Teresa of Avila (1515–82) used to evaluate her visions: they have a sense of power and authority; they produce tranquillity, recollectedness, and a desire to praise God; they impart an inner certainty that what is envisioned is true; they are clear and distinct, with each part carrying great meaning; and finally, the most important criterion, true visions result in a life of improved ethics and psychological integration. They give strength and peace and inspire love for God.[2]

9
The Gift and Burden of Spiritual Awareness

◆◆◆

It is clear from the many accounts of angelic appearances that the person who sees the angel may not necessarily be especially spiritual in outlook. On the other hand, same extremely spiritual people, those who give themselves freely and joyously to the service of God and their fellow creatures, would admit that they have never had an obvious encounter with an angel. In this they would appear to be in good company, for there are many saints commemorated in the Christian calendar whose names one does not immediately associate with angelic communication. Of course, we do not know what occurred in the privacy of their devotional life, but they don't seem to have divulged anything unusual to others. And here, perhaps, we have an important clue.

There are two categories of people most likely to have encountered an angel. First, there is the worldly type of individual who is shocked out of their complacency by a fully materialized apparition that nearly always shows itself during a crisis in their lives. As we have seen earlier, this might be a road accident, a perilous event, or something similar. Alternatively, someone very close to them, whom they believed to be quite well, is shown by an angelic messenger to be desperately ill, or even on the point of death. Their attendance on the dying relative or friend is urgently required. No matter how agnostic they may previously have been, they cannot disown this memorable messenger of help or fate, and the experience may be their way forward to a more considered faith than their previous materialistic assumptions.

The other category of person who is likely to know of angels by firsthand experience is the natural contemplative. In the silence of prayer and the irrepressible joy of being open to the moment in hand, they are available to vast tracts of the cosmos that are a closed book to most other people. In this respect, the cosmos includes not only the astronomical universe, but also the intermediate psychico-spiritual realms that are the preserve of the souls of the departed and the angels of light and darkness. St Paul was well guided when he taught his disciples at Ephesus and Colossae that Christ was the master of this entire realm; we call this manifestation of the Son of God the Cosmic Christ, and his authority and power see to it that all is ultimately well, paradoxically in the present time, no matter how unpleasant things may appear in our little world. It is no wonder either that the natural contemplative has a mystical awareness of the scheme of eternity that includes the angelic hierarchy in its vast form of creation. Such an individual is quite likely to accept the intermediate realm, or dimension, as a matter of course, and work industriously but unobtrusively with the angels of light. These are both invaluable transmitters of divine inspiration and potent allies in a ministry of deliverance. This class of person seldom makes much of an angelic affiliation because it is all so natural; by contrast, the worldly individual who is shaken out of their past preconceptions cannot stop talking about that which they have encountered.

From all this, we may deduce that the dramatic sightings of angels represent only a very small part of a massive whole, too large indeed for us to envisage. The angel is most typical as a formless being who makes its presence felt in the mental processes of the human in terms of inescapable, needle-sharp conscience, irrepressible artistic creativity, and fiercely heroic action in a situation of emergency to the extent that the person's very life may have to be sacrificed. Yet, as we noted in Chapter 4, the angel has idioplastic properties, being able to assume a number of quasi-physical forms. These vary from the classical winged creatures described in Isaiah 6.2–7 and Ezekiel 1.1–13 to apparently well-proportioned and appropriately attired humans who are splendidly helpful in a time of emergency. It is these types of angelic apparitions that, not surprisingly, first make most of us aware of the hierarchy.

While this is all to the good, let it never be forgotten that this form of physical appearance is merely the tip of an enormous iceberg of angelic presence. The typical form of an

angel is spirit and its emanation is light. We remember Jesus'
statement to the Samaritan woman, 'God is spirit, and those
who worship him must worship in spirit and in truth' (John
4.24). We also remember that God is wholly light. The angel
of light shows itself as a spiritual presence of acute illumination
that clears out the inner debris, and replaces it with a freshness
and vigour that speaks of a new life about to burst into the
world to bring it the assurance of redemption and victory over
sin.

How, then, can we become aware of our own guardian angel
to say nothing of the wider ministry around us? The answer is
to love God with all our being and to love our neighbour as
ourself. These 'two great commandments' (Mark 12.29–30)
are our way to the fulfilled life, and in their pursuance as much
of the intermediate dimension will be revealed to us as is right
for us to know. To seek is not good enough in the spiritual
life, for we have also to be inspired by the right motive. If our
motive is merely to satisfy our curiosity or provide us with
psychic power, we are much more likely to effect connection
with the angels of darkness than those of light. This is the
ever-present hazard confronting those who explore what they
call spiritual reality in order simply to acquire greater knowledge.
The process of this somewhat self-centred exploration is loosely
called gnosticism, and it lays open a radical exploration of the
intermediate dimension in order to acquire knowledge, and a
possibly selfish power, over matters of life and death. Gnosis
itself is simply spiritual knowledge, but if it is not pursued
with humility and a desire to serve everyone else, it can
degenerate into a self-willed grasping of the fruit of the tree
of the knowledge of good and evil that Adam and Eve were
forbidden to eat. As I suggested in Chapter 7, God may have
intended them to be seduced by the devil in order to awaken
them to the full knowledge of themselves and the world, but
we do not require this awakening process any longer, because
we should be on the way back to paradise – but now as
responsible adult members of the human race. Spiritual expertise,
misnamed knowledge, in the hands of selfish humans soon
shows itself in distracting psychic phenomena and the practice
of magic (which incidentally is something of a different order

from the sleight-of-hand performed by so-called magicians); this is indeed the practical end of gnosticism.

A truly spiritual person would not be diverted by such a degraded and futile activity, simply because they would be moving in a very different field of experience. Indeed, once we know something of the heavenly banquet mentioned in various passages of the Bible, especially Luke 14.16–24, earthly fare (and here I allude to psychical phenomena) has a very bland taste. Another way of putting the same observation is, 'Set your mind on God's kingdom and his justice before everything else, and all the rest will come to you as well' (Matthew 6.33). This injunction of Jesus applies not only to the things of this world but also to hidden, or occult, matters that so easily become the domain of the antichrist, unless we treat them with chastity and reverence.

Nothing in God's creation is wrong by nature; it is what we humans do with it that makes it dangerous, or even depraved. I mentioned in Chapter 7 that even demonic spirits may be under obedience to evil humanity, and the first part of their redemption is to be freed from these predatory monsters. I am also reminded of Martin Buber's observation interpreting Hasidism (a mystical movement of Eastern European Jews starting in the eighteenth century): 'There is no not-holy, there is only that which has not yet been hallowed, which has not been redeemed to its holiness.'[1] If a person is centred on God, and especially the person of Christ, they do not require a deep knowledge of hidden things; instead, these are shown to them as the occasion and necessity arises. A person who is not centred on the Divine tends to cling to fragments of esoteric doctrine rather like a drowning sailor hanging on to pieces of wreckage in a stormy sea.

The lives of a number of medieval saints have been punctuated by angelic encounters, the most outstanding of which have been those of Joan of Arc, who was inspired by the archangel Michael in her military campaigns to liberate France from English domination, and St Francis of Assisi, who had many meetings with angels in the course of his holy life. I must confess, however, that when I read the history of some of the saints of yore and the angelic helpers that appeared repeatedly in the course of their work, I begin to feel a trifle uneasy, even irritated. This reaction could certainly be one of deep-seated envy, but I dislike displays of exhibitionism, especially of a religious type.

If one is sensitive to the deeper moral issues of any one period, one will not fail to hear the inner voice of one's own guardian angel. Therefore the essential requirement for angelic communication is the practice of silence, an unstudied silence in which one can be absolutely available to the demands of the present moment, the passing scene. Such a silence makes one alert to what God wants of one, and the information is transmitted by an angel, whether one's own guardian, or another one, or both acting together. (I would not care to conjecture on this.) This is why the sentimental accounts of angelic visitations in the past, or for that matter the present, to especially holy people do not especially attract me. If one is the recipient of angelic communication, it is certainly wiser to conceal the matter lest one becomes arrogant, believing one is holier than the rest of humanity.

There may be special occasions when a disclosure is important, but one should be aware of what one is doing. It is quite in order to discuss an apparition with an expert in the field so as to set one's mind at rest, because there is always the possibility that one is mentally disturbed and the angelic figure is really a pathological type of hallucination. The general demeanour of the person who has had the apparition is a good working guide in this matter of discernment. If there is a degree of psychic inflation, with the person thinking that they are especially important in the scheme of things, it is more probable that they are being afflicted by a demonic spirit – in other words, an angel of darkness.

After Jesus had performed his many healing miracles, he requested the grateful person to present himself or herself to the priest, and make the offering laid down by Moses for their cleansing (Leviticus 14.1–32), as in the case of so-called leprosy (Mark 1.40–4), but he enjoined them to tell no one else. Hence Mark's Gospel is sometimes especially associated with the 'messianic secret', though this is encountered in Matthew and Luke also. This type of secrecy is good when one has had a deep spiritual experience – let it be known only to one's immediate circle, and then let the matter drop, except of course from one's own memory. Mary herself treasured in her heart all the things that happened to Jesus during his stay at home when he was preparing for his great ministry (Luke 2.51). Yet in the end it was brought to a glorious fulfilment in his ministry, passion, death, and resurrection. In other words, the validity of an angelic encounter is proved by the subsequent life of the individual; the same applies to any truly spiritual experience. A psychic experience makes one wonder, and this is potentially a very good thing, but a spiritual experience transforms one into something of the holiness that is an impress of the Divine on the soul.

It is an invariable rule that the class of contemplative who has seen angels of light must also be prepared to be accosted by demonic spirits. This rule depends on the innate sensitivity of the person. It must be said also that some distinctly worldly people have an innate psychic sensitivity that makes them easy victims of demonic assault; the work of the spiritual director with such people is to open them to the spiritual dimension of reality, so that what started as a grave problem can eventually become a major blessing. People on the path of spiritual development must be prepared to be assaulted by demonic forces. This is not merely a malicious prank on the part of these forces, but also an indication of the work ahead of such people. The forces of darkness, I believe, seek their own salvation, which they may indeed attain when their work in the advancement of the universe has been completed. It is very unpleasant to be assailed by a demonic spirit, as I indicated in Chapter 7, but one does not lose if one keeps one's faith and remains courageous. Just as we do not grow physically on a diet of water, so our spiritual development depends on our mastery of the various elements in our physical and psychical environment. St Paul found his Corinthian converts so un-spiritual that he had, figuratively, to feed them on milk rather than solid food. He had to deal with them on the natural plane, as infants in Christ. They were not ready for the solid food of spiritual doctrine because they were still full of jealousy, strife, and partisanship (I Corinthians 3.1–4). A little pain adds the age of experience rapidly to one's score of years.

In the eighty-fourth dialogue of *Talking with Angels*,[2] there is the provoking teaching: 'Suffering teaches nothing and suffering does not redeem. There is no need for suffering.' On the surface this sounds quite wrong, because we learn by experience, and suffering is a most important part of our own reaction to unpleasant circumstances. But the solution to this seeming paradox soon follows: 'Blows and punishment need not be: suffering need not be! *Giving of oneself, sacrifice, extinguishes it.* This is the most sacred Grace.' The italicized portion is as in the original. Demonic assault teaches one that one's life is a gift of God for the whole community. Recalling Hillel's aphorism once more, we are to care first of all for our own good, and then bequeath that accumulated good to our fellow creatures. If we are unwise enough to keep all our riches to ourselves, they are likely to turn cancerous. If we are wise, we remember William Blake's poem from *Auguries of Innocence*:

> A truth that's told with bad intent
> Beats all the lies you can invent;
> It is right it should be so.
> Man was made for joy and woe,
> And when this we rightly know
> Through the world we safely go.
> Joy and woe are woven fine,
> A clothing for the soul divine.
> Under every grief and pine
> Runs a joy of silken twine.[3]

This juxtaposition of good and bad is part of the nature of life: the bad pushes us onwards, while the good gives us a time of blessing and release when we can bestow our accumulated gifts on those around us. But were there no onward movement with all the toil it involves, there would be few gifts to provide at the end of the day. Therefore an authentic angelic recipient is fully aware of the dark side of life, as revealed by the demonic spirits. Furthermore, such a person is undeterred by the darkness and is able to spread the light ever more radiantly as their life progresses. The golden aureole that painters of olden times portrayed above the heads of the saints is a real depiction of this light. If one knows God, a knowledge never to be taken for granted by even the holiest person (not that such a person would ever make that assumption), one can always know of the light that transcends all darkness, of which we read in John I.5, 'The light shines in the darkness, and the darkness has never mastered it.'

To see the cosmos as intrinsically friendly, even when we are apparently in mortal danger, is a great gift of understanding. It is our own fear and the hatred this engenders that is the real enemy. The cosmic forces are frequently terrifying in their intensity, but if we hold fast to God in unceasing prayer, we shall come through and be able to give our special gifts to the world. A state of unceasing prayer is one in which we are never far from the remembrance of God at any time of our life, day and night, waking and sleeping. Periods set aside specially for prayer are very important, since during this time we are able to come close to God by a deliberate giving of ourself and an openness to his grace. The more assiduously we practise this discipline, the sooner we will attain a state of unceasing prayer. The world's company of saints are our greatest inspiration as practitioners of prayer that fulfils itself in service to the community, which may vary from works of charity to ceaseless intercession for all God's creatures.

I like the observation by Goethe: 'Even Mme de Staël was shocked because I had made God the Father so friendly to the Devil ... What will she say if she meets him again in a higher sphere, perhaps even in heaven itself?' The basis of this remark was the drama *Faust*, immortalized, if not created, by Goethe. A consideration of this theme is contained in an observation made by F. Melian Stawell and G. Lowes Dickinson:

> Faust reacts and reaches safety, not only in spite of, but actually because of, Mephistopheles' influence. For Mephistopheles, though he revolts against the light, is all the same, as he knows himself, a portion of 'the Darkness that brought the Light to birth'. And that is one reason why, as the drama proceeds and Faust begins to learn, Mephistopheles appears

less and less as the tempter and more and more as the instrument of Faust's creative purpose. He bets with God in the Prologue that he will destroy Faust, but from the very beginning it is made clear that he will not win his bet. For by his fundamental nature he cannot help contributing to Faust's progress.[4]

The fate of the world, maybe even the universe, depends on God's central piece, the human. No one can shrug off the appalling evil humans have committed against their own kind, against nature, and ultimately against themselves personally. If they progress on their own without reference to God, however he may be named, the more certain is their self-destruction. If, on the other hand, they are open to the intermediate dimension and the power of the Holy Spirit, they could experience a great leap forward. The end would be 'Christ consciousness', which would lead to a liberation of the whole world from the shackles of mortality and its entry upon the 'glorious liberty of the children of God', to quote Romans 8.21 once more. The sooner we are brave enough to extend the range of human knowledge from the limits of the reasoning mind and are open to larger possibilities relating to angels and all that pertains to them, the more rapidly will we be able to move onwards towards the vision of God from whom all blessings flow. Then indeed a new race of humans will appear, true representatives all in their own way of the Lord Jesus himself.

NOTES

1 ANGELS IN A MYSTICAL CONTEXT

1 *The Cloud of Unknowing*, chapter 6.
2 Dionysius the Areopagite, *On Mystical Theology* and *The Celestial Hierarchies* (The Editors of the Shrine of Wisdom, Fintry, Brook, Godalming, Surrey, 1961). (Earlier translations followed the Latin titles *De Mystica Theologia* and *De Caelesti Ierarchia*.)

4 THE EXPERIENCE OF ANGELS

1 M. Israel, *The Quest for Wholeness* (Darton, Longman & Todd, London, 1989).
2 P. W. Martin, *Experiment in Depth* (Routledge and Kegan Paul, London, 1955), pp. 162–3.
3 J. Danielou, *The Angels and Their Mission* (Christian Classics, Westminster, Maryland, 1987).

5 THE PROPERTIES OF ANGELS

1 M. Parisen, ed., *Angels and Mortals: Their Co-creative Power* (Quest Books, Wheaton, Illinois, 1994).
2 The details of the apparitions at Fatima and Garabandal are found in P. Giovetti, *Angels: The Role of Celestial Guardians and Beings of Light* (Samuel Weiser Inc., North Beach, Maine, 1993), pp. 92–6. A useful book about Medjugorje is J. Ashton, *The People's Madonna: An Account of the Visions of Mary at Medjugorje* (HarperCollins, London, 1991). Another useful text about visitations of the Virgin Mary is J. Ashton, *Mother of All Nations: The Visitations of the Blessed Virgin Mary and Her Message for Today* (Harper & Row, San Francisco, 1989).
3 F. Thompson, *Collected Poems* (Fisher Press, Sevenoaks, Kent, 1992), p. 286.
4 *Poetical Works of Robert Bridges* (Oxford University Press, London, 1936), p. 291.
5 R. M. Rilke, *Duino Elegies*, trs. S. Cohn (Carcanet, Manchester, 1989), pp. 21, 27, 29, 73, 75.
6 R. M. Rilke, *Sonnets to Orpheus*, trs. M. D. Herter (Norton, New York and London, W. W. Norton & Co., 1962, 1992) pp. 135–6.

7 F. Copleston, *History of Philosophy: Medieval Philosophy*, vol. II, pt. 2, (Search Press, London, 1979), p. 329.

8 J. Daniélou, *Recherches des Sciences Religieuses* (XLV, 1957), pp. 5–41. 'Trinité et Angélologie dans la Théologie Judéo-crétien'.

9 P. Tillich, *Systematic Theology*, vol. I (University of Chicago Press, Chicago, 1951; first published in Great Britain by Nisbet, 1953), p. 289.

10 P. Tillich, *A History of Christian Thought* (SCM Press, London, 1968), p. 94.

11 D. Miller, 'Theologia Imaginalis', in Parisen, *Angels and Mortals*.

6 ANGELS OF DARKNESS

1 A useful book concerning some of these matters is by the Christian Exorcism Study Group, edited by M. Perry, *Deliverance: Psychic Disturbances and Occult Involvement* (SPCK, London, 1987).

7 THE LIGHT AND THE DARKNESS

1 R. Assagioli, *Psychosynthesis* (Turnstone Press, Wellingborough, 1986), p. 144.

2 M. Israel, *Precarious Living* (Mowbray, Oxford, 1982).

8 THE TEACHING QUALITY OF ANGELS

1 G. Mallasz, *Talking with Angels* (Daimon Verlag, Einsiedeln, Switzerland, 1992).

2 For further reading on St Teresa of Avila, see D. Green, *Gold in the Crucible: Teresa of Avila and the Western Mystical Tradition* (Element Books, Shaftesbury, Dorset, 1989), pp. 56–8.

9 THE GIFT AND BURDEN OF SPIRITUAL AWARENESS

1 M. Buber, *Hasidism* (Philosophical Library, New York). Quoted in V. Gollancz, *A Year of Grace* (Victor Gollancz, London, 1950), p. 96.

2 G. Mallasz, *Talking with Angels* (Daimon Verlag, Einsiedeln, Switzerland, 1992).

3 From M. Mason, ed., *William Blake: A Critical Edition of the Major Works* (Oxford University Press, Oxford, 1988), p. 29.

4 The quotations from Goethe and about Faust come from F. Melian Stawell and G. Lowes Dickinson, *Goethe and Faust* (Bell, London, 1928), pp. 67 and 69.

FURTHER READING

The following books are helpful as a general resource for the study of angels:

Hope Price, *Angels: True Stories of How They Touch Our Lives* (Macmillan, London, 1993). This is a good account of various types of angelic apparitions recorded by refreshingly balanced people.

Paola Giovetti, tr. Toby McCormick, *Angels: The Role of Celestial Guardians and Beings of Light* (Samuel Weiser Inc., North Beach, Maine, 1993). This book contains a useful account of angels, including some descriptions of apparitions. It starts with the orthodox Christian view, and then extends to other more esoteric fields of enquiry. There are some good coloured pictures depicting angels.

Maria Parisen, ed., *Angels and Mortals: Their Co-creative Power* (Quest Books, Wheaton, Illinois, 1994). This book is a series of separate articles collected over a period of time. Quest Books is part of the Theosophical Publishing House; thus this particular book is bound to have its quota of unorthodox material. This does not, in my opinion, detract from its value; rather, it will probably open up new ways of thought to the diligent reader, who may indeed disagree, as I do, with some of the contents. However, the overall value is profound. Articles I especially recommend are:
'The Nature of Angel Forms', by G. Don Gilmore, pp. 7–17;
'On Re-imaging Angels', by Jay G. Williams, pp. 18–31;
'The Cult of the Guardian Angel', by Michael Grosso, pp. 125–38;
'Theologia Imaginalis', by David L. Miller, pp. 157–76;
'Temperance: Heavenly Alchemist', by Sallie Nichols, pp. 189–200.